Targeting in Social Programs

Targeting in Social Programs

Avoiding Bad Bets,
Removing Bad Apples

Peter H. Schuck

Richard J. Zeckhauser

BROOKINGS INSTITUTION PRESS
Washington, D.C.

Copyright © 2006
THE BROOKINGS INSTITUTION
1775 Massachusetts Avenue, N.W., Washington, D.C. 20036
www.brookings.edu

Library of Congress Cataloging-in-Publication data

Schuck, Peter H.
    Targeting in social programs : avoiding bad bets, removing bad apples / Peter H. Schuck, Richard J. Zeckhauser.
        p. cm.
    Summary: "Provides a framework for analyzing the challenges involved in defining bad bets and bad apples and discusses the safeguards that any classification process must provide. Examines public schools, public housing, and medical care and proposes policy changes that could reduce the problems these two groups pose in social welfare programs"—Provided by publisher.
    Includes bibliographical references and index.
    ISBN-13: 978-0-8157-7880-6 (cloth : alk. paper)
    ISBN-10: 0-8157-7880-5 (cloth : alk. paper)
    1. Public welfare administration—United States. 2. Human services—Government policy—United States. 3. United States—Social policy—1993–. I. Zeckhauser, Richard. II. Title.
    HV95.S38 2006
    361.6'120973—dc22   2006029184

9 8 7 6 5 4 3 2 1

The paper used in this publication meets minimum requirements of the American National Standard for Information Sciences—Permanence of Paper for Printed Library Materials: ANSI Z39.48-1992.

Typeset in Adobe Garamond

Composition by Kulamer Publishing Services
Potomac, Maryland

Printed by R. R. Donnelley
Harrisonburg, Virginia

We dedicate this work to our wives,
Marcy and Sally,
and to a Schuck–Zeckhauser friendship
that stretches over 50 years.

Contents

Acknowledgments

This book could not have been written without the assistance of many people and institutions. We benefited from comments, constructive even when skeptical, from fellow scholars including Henry Aaron, Richard Arum, David Cutler, Jack Donahue, Lee Ann Fennell, Christopher Jencks, Ron Haskins, Jeffrey Liebman, and Benjamin Sommers, as well as from participants in seminars at Harvard's Kennedy School of Government and the law schools at New York University, Yale, and the University of Georgia where we presented earlier versions of our work. Special thanks go to David Super for reading several chapters and improving our presentation. Two wise medical practitioners, Dr. Samuel Osher and Dr. Randy Reinhold, pointed us in fruitful directions, and our investigations of agency practices in New York City, presented in chapter 5, were facilitated by public officials identified in the notes. Outstanding and extensive research assistance was provided by Melissa Cox (herself a Brookings co-author), who was assisted at one point by Joey Fishkin—both members of the Yale Law School class of 2007. Anda Bordean, Deanna Dong, Felipe Kast, and Nils Wernerfelt, all Harvard students, effectively undertook specific research tasks. Miriam Avins used her deft pen to greatly strengthen the final product. At Brookings Institution Press, Chris Kelaher shepherded our book through the approval process, Mary Kwak gave us insightful editing suggestions, and Anthony Nathe scrupulously edited our copy. Wendy Wyatt tended our manuscript with her usual skill. Finally, we thank our great institutions—Yale, NYU, and Harvard—for their support.

Please see our website www.ksg.harvard.edu/fs/rzeckhauser/targetingin socialprograms.htm.

Targeting in Social Programs

1

Introduction

This book has a simple and straightforward message. The political and programmatic success of social programs requires improved target efficiency: directing resources where they do the most good. Although this fact is widely understood, it is seldom discussed, much less analyzed—and certainly not by the supporters of such programs. Our principal goal in writing this book is to make that discussion more coherent, better informed, and easier to conduct.

The public domain boasts many sound social programs. Some of these programs seek to allocate resources to individuals who are members of a legally defined target group—people whom politicians and policymakers have chosen to receive these resources. But many social programs are not nearly as well targeted as they could be, and a few are so poorly targeted as to call their social value into serious question. Public policy should improve the targeting of social programs so that they can accomplish more of their goals while using the same resources to assist the same needy populations.

We are particularly concerned with programs that seek to improve the conditions and opportunities of unfortunate, disadvantaged, usually low-income individuals, people whom we call *bad draws*.[1] We think of these bad draws as parties to a kind of

1

social contract for insurance against certain random misfortunes. This is why the government pays for medical care for the sick, unemployment benefits for those who lose their jobs, and food stamps for those who would otherwise be hungry or malnourished.

The category of bad draws, of course, is extremely broad, providing little guidance to policymakers who must allocate social welfare resources among the many bad draws who have plausible claims on society's solicitude. This book seeks to provide better guidance by focusing on two particular groups of bad draws who divert resources from the other bad draws for whom they were primarily intended. We call these two groups *bad bets* and *bad apples*. All of the individuals in these two groups are bad draws, but they are not well-targeted beneficiaries, either because they derive little benefit from a program (bad bets) or because their very participation imposes significant costs on other participants (bad apples).

Bad bets are individuals who are likely to benefit little from social resources relative to other bad draws. Our paradigmatic bad bet is a chronically ill nonagenarian who receives costly medical treatments at public expense, which predictably will yield little social benefit.

Bad apples are individuals whose irresponsible, immoral, or illegal behavior in the past—and predictably, in the future as well—marks them as unsuitable to receive the benefits of social programs.[2] We are concerned in this book with a subset of this category: those who interfere with the ability of deserving participants to benefit from a program. (Most bad apples also harm themselves, but our principal concern here is their adverse effect on *good apples* in the same programs.) An all-too-common example of a bad apple is the public school student who chronically disrupts class and thereby impairs the learning of others who desperately need a sound education. Another bad apple is the public housing tenant or homeless-shelter resident whose repeated misconduct debases his or her neighbors' quality of life. Bad apples are found in every segment of society; the category includes many who are relatively wealthy and advantaged (*good draws*).[3] Here, however, we focus on bad apples who are bad draws because they are the ones who consume the scarce resources available for important social welfare programs.

Bad bets and bad apples pose distinct challenges to policymakers, but we think it is useful to address them in a single book. We are keenly aware of the many hard issues raised by a serious effort to understand and address these two problems. First, merely defining these two categories of program beneficiaries is a profoundly difficult undertaking, necessitating tough line-drawing decisions. Second, an even more controversial challenge is the administrative task of assigning particular beneficiaries to these categories. This process in effect labels some individuals as socially or programmatically undesirable (in the case of bad apples), and others as relatively unlikely to benefit from program resources (in the case of bad bets). Third, each of these judgments entails predicting future behavior or events on the basis of inevitably limited information, which makes some level of error inescapable. Implementing such judgments in the real world of program administration raises many challenges. Fourth, to make matters worse, we cannot precisely measure the social benefits of avoiding bad bets or removing bad apples, nor can we measure the likely costs of implementing policies that do so. Finally, the politics of dealing forthrightly and effectively with the problems posed by these two groups—or indeed, even candidly acknowledging these problems—are bound to be daunting. We strongly suspect that the sense of futility that many policymakers feel at the prospect of openly confronting these problems helps to explain why they have received relatively little attention. All the more reason, then, for academics like us to get the analytical ball rolling.

The book proceeds as follows. In chapter 2, we present the foundations of our analytical approach and introduce the subject of target efficiency, which is pivotal to this approach. We elaborate on the definitions and the positive, normative, and methodological assumptions that guide our discussion, and we highlight the most difficult issues raised by our analysis. In addition, we address a very hard question: what should social programs do with the bad bets they avoid or the bad apples they remove? This presentation, while longer than we would like, is essential to understanding what follows.

In chapter 3, we begin with an analysis of the stakes facing social policymakers, whom we urge to think more rigorously and courageously about bad bets and bad apples. We then explain the reluctance of politicians and bureaucrats to acknowledge and deal with the problems posed by bad apples and bad bets. This reluctance ends up harming precisely those bad draws who most deserve the help of social programs: individuals who are both good apples and good bets. We then present a taxonomy of bad policies—some handicapped by poor targeting, others exhibiting different flaws—and conclude by analyzing six pathologies that contribute to poor targeting across a wide range of social programs.

Citizens who want to maintain and expand social programs designed to promote the well-being of deserving bad draws have an important stake in avoiding bad bets and removing bad apples. We call such citizens *well-targeted redistributionists*, and we count ourselves among them. Well-targeted redistributionists should want to recapture the resources squandered on bad apples and bad bets so that they can be redirected to better purposes. Alas, as we explain, many well-targeted redistributionists impede this goal (sometimes naively) by pretending that bad apples and bad bets scarcely exist and ignoring the misallocation problems that these groups present. In this way, the redistributionists make it that much easier for politicians and bureaucrats to engage in the same neglect.

In chapters 4 and 5, respectively, we develop the analysis of bad bets and bad apples in considerable detail. These chapters examine several social program areas to help provide the focus and data needed for clearer thinking about improving targeting. For bad bets, health care examples get primary attention, largely because of the enormous amounts of money involved. For bad apples, our main examples are welfare programs, school classrooms, public housing, and homeless shelters.

As noted earlier, classifying an eligible beneficiary as a bad bet or a bad apple can require very difficult and controversial predictions of future events and behavior. In chapter 6, we examine the subject of target efficiency in more detail, focusing on three distinct targeting processes: sorting by authorities, sorting by recipients, and sorting with appeals. The difficulties of prediction and classification are discussed, as well as the procedural protections that are essential to making these decisions with acceptable levels of accuracy and fairness.

In chapter 7, we highlight the central themes of the book by considering the steps policymakers must take to improve program targeting. The first step is to obtain better information about individuals and programs. The second is to apply our methods to specific cases. We illustrate this process with several examples and conclude the chapter and the book by urging policymakers to employ both caution and urgency as they seek to improve target efficiency.

The basic goal of target efficiency—allocating resources to the individuals for whom and the purposes for which they will do the most good—is straightforward and should not be controversial. Nevertheless, this goal often proves elusive. Giving resources to A but not to B, or putting them toward goal X but not toward goal Y, immediately raises a host of challenges—some conceptual or analytical, but many of them purely political. For example, those who represent B will protest and may even sue. Even more vociferous will be the groups that deliver resources to B or sell services in support of Y. For example, organizations that purport to speak for low-income people often oppose removing bad apple tenants from public housing and bad apple students from traditional schools, while the good apple beneficiaries to whom these programs are targeted prefer that the disrupters be removed.

Conservatives are likely to be skeptical of any effort to improve targeting that they fear may be costly. Indeed, they may think that a poorly functioning social welfare system better serves their efforts to discredit the welfare state and limit its expenditures. Liberals, for their part, seldom actively champion target efficiency. As we discuss in chapters 3 and 5, they tend to worry that acknowledging the problem of bad apples amounts to blaming the victim, maligning the poor, and undermining the legitimacy of cherished social programs. They exhibit a particular and seldom discussed (much less publicly defended) form of risk aversion: to draw on a cliché from criminal law, they would rather serve ten undeserving recipients than deny a single deserving one.

Expecting little sympathy for target efficiency from either end of the political spectrum, we look for support from well-targeted redistributionists, who cluster in the middle and who, we suspect, vastly outnumber those at the left and right extremes.[4] We expect that their willingness to devote resources to education, health care, low-income housing, rehabilitation of prisoners, and other social welfare programs would expand significantly if the target efficiency of such programs improved—that is, if they weeded out the chronically disruptive students, the patients getting little benefit from vast Medicaid and Medicare expenditures, the public housing and homeless shelter residents who spoil their neighbors' quality of life, and the recidivist criminals.

Liberals and conservatives should both want to spend money where it will accomplish the most good, without seriously undermining beneficiaries' incentives to improve their own status. We are encouraged in this expectation by the overwhelming public approval of the efforts to improve targeting in welfare programs that began in the mid-1990s—first with experimental state programs and then through the 1996 federal welfare reform law. The government now spends far more money per capita for support of the good apple poor than it did before the reforms were adopted, and politicians' attacks on the newer welfare programs are much reduced. For well-targeted redistributionists, this is good news indeed.

This book presents considerable empirical data to document the problems it explores. Little of that data is new, however, other than the tallies of media mentions of "welfare fraud" and "welfare recipient" in chapter 3 and the information, detailed in chapter 5, that we report from the agencies that deal with public schools, public housing, and homeless shelters in New York City. We recognize that these reports are neither rigorous nor systematic, but they do illustrate the nature and magnitude of the challenges raised by the bad apples problem and suggest some approaches that policymakers might take. Our main contribution, then, is not to adduce new data but rather to present a framework for thinking about social policy that has not come naturally to those engaged in policy debates or administering social programs. The data, examples, and analyses that we provide show how this framework could and should apply in the design and implementation of social programs.

Some readers will criticize one or another example. Others will insist that even repeated misbehavior does not mean that one is a bad apple. Still others will maintain that it is wrong to exclude people of certain ages or medical conditions from public benefits simply because they are bad bets. Others will dispute our empirical claims—for example, that removing chronically disruptive students will improve the life chances of those who remain. These factual issues are highly relevant to sound policymaking, but we do not propose to debate, much less resolve, them here. Our goal, rather, is to establish sound policy precepts.

Policymakers should be eager to refine the specific examples that we cite and to learn about other examples that would help them to improve targeting in their programs. Again, our chief purpose is to establish sound principles and then provide examples that can help test their plausibility. Readers who find our framework useful should test it in their own policy domains. We imagine, for example, that thinking about antipoverty programs in terms of bad draws, bad bets, and bad apples could extend the lessons of the 1996 welfare reform, discussed in chapters 3 and 5, to a broader array of both actual and proposed social problems and interventions. By systematically developing the framework presented here, we hope to make the tough choices entailed by efforts to improve targeting in social policy more analytical, more accessible, and thus more thinkable.

2

Conceptual Foundations of Target Efficiency

In chapter 1, we presented preliminary definitions of some of the concepts that will figure centrally in our analysis of target efficiency in social programs. In this chapter, we elaborate on and refine these concepts, add some important ideas, make explicit the assumptions and methodology that will guide this analysis, and consider what should happen to the bad bets who are avoided and the bad apples who are removed under our approach.

Definitions and Concepts

Bad draws are people who were dealt a bad hand at birth or later and who have suffered misfortune as a result. (We also refer to bad draws by the more familiar term "disadvantaged.") Modern welfare states like the United States characteristically design social programs to alleviate the suffering of many (but not all) kinds of bad draws.[1] The vast majority of the bad draws whom these programs benefit are both good apples and good bets, which is why taxpayers support the programs. Better targeting can increase this support and more effectively alleviate suffering, as we show in chapter 3.

Bad bets, the subject of chapter 4, are people who are unlikely to derive much benefit from a programmatic intervention on their behalf relative to either the resources that they would consume or the benefits that better bets would derive from the same resources. A common example of a bad bet who would gain too little benefit compared with what another beneficiary would gain is a person in precarious health competing with a far healthier person for a cadaver kidney. The current priority system for kidneys in the United States, holding constant quality-of-match, allocates them first to the individuals who have been waiting the longest, and who are often the sickest. As a result, it often targets kidneys to those who will receive the least benefit from them (in quality-adjusted life years).[2]

The more common kind of bad bet, however, is an individual who will derive too little benefit relative to the material resources he or she consumes. An elderly person in poor condition is a low-value candidate for an expensive heart valve transplant, even though heart valves, while costly, are readily available. A college student who is likely to drop out is a bad bet for heavily subsidized higher education. One who has already dropped out of high school is an even worse bet, yet remarkably, this bet is one that public colleges are increasingly making.[3]

Bad bets, then, are a concern for policymakers because bad bets consume program resources that could be better directed to other bad draws. As we discuss in chapters 3 and 4, this constitutes a widespread form of social waste. Although even poor targeting will generate at least some benefits and may also increase political support for a program (indeed, that is the purpose of much poor targeting; examples are given in chapter 7), the overall costs of poor targeting are often higher than what society wishes or needs to bear.

Some program beneficiaries are bad bets because of a widely accepted distributional norm, such as progressivity, under which society thinks that other less advantaged members of the target group would derive more benefit from the same resources. Tax expenditure policies and other programs targeted at the wealthy—frequently in disguised fashion—often include beneficiaries who will produce little or no policy bang for the buck. Farm subsidies provide an important example. Despite the populist rhetoric that surrounds them, they primarily benefit giant agribusinesses, not family farms.[4] Similarly, the tax deduction of mortgage interest for second homes, including very expensive ones, disproportionately benefits the wealthy, who would probably buy their homes in any event.[5] Since we wish to focus on programs for bad draws, we say little at this point about programs that target poorly in that they primarily help good draws. We discuss this problem and present additional examples in chapter 7.

Bad apples, the subject of chapter 5, are very different: they may or may not be bad bets except insofar as their past misconduct predicts future recidivism. Most bad apples are chronic, serious disrupters of the programs in which they participate, and they do more than simply waste scarce program resources. Their immoral, irresponsible, or illegal conduct also reduces the degree to which good apple participants benefit from a program. In addition, some bad apples harm good apples more indirectly by causing taxpayers to stigmatize the entire group and thus the program more generally in ways that erode its public support. (We discuss the relation among bad apples, stigma, and taxpayer attitudes later in this chapter and also in chapter 5 and take up the challenges of accurate prediction and classification, as well as procedural design, in chapter 6.) Bad apples who engage in fraud and abuse in social programs also generate stigma and create other serious programmatic and political problems. But for reasons explained in chapter 5, this book focuses on the more numerous bad apples whose misconduct (chronic disruptive behavior, for example) may fall short of crime or fraud and therefore receives much less attention from policymakers.

The factors that lead an individual to become a bad apple are often complex and sometimes even beyond his or her control. Thus, the very idea of labeling an individual, particularly a schoolchild or other young person, as a bad apple will strike many readers as harsh, even repellent. Their unease may be heightened by the fact that for purposes of our analysis, we treat these factors as irrelevant to the classification—so long as program administrators (for example, school or public housing officials) cannot rectify those causes through the kinds of conventional, short-term interventions that are ordinarily at their disposal. In chapter 5, we take up the plausible and common objection that—regardless of the accuracy of the classification and the fairness of the procedures (the subjects of chapter 6)—labeling individuals as bad apples (not to mention removing them from social programs) amounts to "blaming the victim." This objection, we show, misses the main point, which is to accord the highest social priority to improving outcomes for good apples, while also attempting to address directly the reasons for bad apples.

This priority may require separating the bad apples from the good ones until they have reformed and will no longer harm others in the program—perhaps after rehabilitation of some kind. Like us, many voters refer to such disrupters colloquially as bad apples while supporting programs designed to separate and rehabilitate them and, it is hoped, return them to the mainstream. This is not inconsistent. Indeed, using the term bad apples in this same firmly judgmental but optimistically redemptive spirit is probably a key to finding effective ways to remedy their difficult problems.

Some people who consume significant program resources do not fit easily into either the bad bet or bad apple category, yet they also pose daunting, important challenges for policymakers. We briefly discuss three of these special categories here—self-spoilers, group stigmatizers, and resource drains. We then discuss the potential overlap between bad bets and bad apples.

Self-Spoilers

Certain beneficiaries of social programs may have ended up in the same penurious, unhealthy, disabled, or other exigent circumstances as others who receive program benefits, yet we may want to treat them differently because they have brought their harm upon themselves. To put the point another way, they have created their own bad draws. By exacerbating their own problems, either in the short or long term, they may defeat the purposes of the social programs designed to benefit them.[6] For example, self-spoilers may decide not to work or to care for themselves although they are capable of work or self-care. They may chronically misbehave in school or drop out at an early age, thus severely limiting their future job opportunities. They may engage in irresponsible sexual conduct that produces children whom they do not want or whom they will leave to others to raise (possibly public or state-funded private agencies). In chapters 4 and 5, we discuss some other examples of self-spoilers, including Mickey Mantle, who despite many rehabilitation programs destroyed his liver through chronic alcohol abuse.

Social welfare programs intended to help the poor sometimes perversely harm them by encouraging self-spoiling conduct—a form of moral hazard discussed in later chapters. When this happens, the self-destructive behavior may become contagious, as it becomes more acceptable and then spreads into more widespread use. "Defining deviancy down" (as the late Daniel Patrick Moynihan famously termed it) debases public values by normalizing previously condemned conduct.[7] This normalization encourages others to engage in similar conduct, to society's detriment. The sharp increase in out-of-wedlock births from the 1960s to the 1990s is a particularly tragic example of this phenomenon. (This can also occur at the higher-income end of the social ladder, as seen in the increased doping among successful professional athletes and the contagious use of illegal tax shelters and shady accounting practices by the wealthy.) By the same token, appropriate reforms can engender a virtuous cycle. In chapters 3 and 5, we suggest that welfare reform may have had this meliorative effect. By lifting the aspirations of their neighbors (broadly defined), self-improvers may have helped to foster the postwelfare reform decline in illegitimacy rates and chronic unemployment among the poor.

Society may wish to treat self-spoilers less generously than it treats other bad draws whose disadvantage is not self-inflicted, for several reasons. First, self-spoilers are likely to be bad bets. We expect that self-spoilers will derive less benefit from resources than will other people with similar needs, because the self-spoilers have caused their own problems and may do so again. Second, we may believe that those who cause their own disadvantage are less deserving of social resources—whether the resource be tragically scarce (as was the liver given to Mantle) or fiscally scarce (as are cash transfers). Someone with lung cancer who took up smoking in the last twenty years, long after its causal relationship with lung cancer was firmly established, has less of a moral claim on society's solicitude, and hence on the resources required for an expensive treatment, than does an individual like Dana Reeve, whose lung cancer was not self-inflicted through smoking. Third, we may worry about the perverse incentives that giving resources to self-spoilers creates. Even if they would benefit enough from the program to be worthwhile from a cost-effectiveness perspective, this might attract other people to the self-destructive behavior. If so, self-spoilers would be like bad apples in that they harm otherwise good apples. Indeed, if incentive effects were sufficiently strong, then providing benefits to self-spoilers might even generate negative quality-adjusted life years on balance. (Quality-adjusted life years, often abbreviated QALYs, is our outcome measure for medical interventions. We discuss it at length in chapter 4.)

Self-spoilers, of course, may demand equal treatment with "pure" bad draws on the grounds that they drew a bad hand in being born with a propensity to self-spoiling. More "traditional" bad apples, we have seen, can also claim this excuse. However, these bad apples harm others whereas self-spoilers largely harm themselves. For this reason, we treat self-spoilers as a distinct category of bad bets in chapter 4, while recognizing that they share some features with bad apples.

Group Stigmatizers

Bad apples often harm a social program by bringing its other beneficiaries into disrepute. The spread of this stigma tends to confirm advocates' worst fears about the program's political vulnerability. The adage that a relatively few bad apples can spoil the barrel, blighting the lives and opportunities of the vastly larger number of good apples whom outsiders cannot easily distinguish is clearly true. And observers tend to homogenize probabilities, failing to distinguish whether 1 percent of a pool consists of bad apples or whether their share is 10 percent.[8]

It is easy to see why observers fall into this error. Few people accurately assess the probabilities of complex phenomena, relying instead on cognitive shortcuts. For example, a phenomenon seems much more prevalent if one can bring a particular instance to mind—what psychologists call the "availability heuristic."[9] When politicians or other opinion leaders denounce the misconduct of someone like Willy Horton or a "welfare queen," we tend to imagine that this misconduct is more common than it actually is. The public image of the events at Abu Ghraib did not depend much on whether prisoners were abused by three soldiers or thirty, or whether there were thirty or three hundred soldiers guarding them. The vivid photographs were enough to arouse widespread disgust and to create a perception that abuse was common. Journalists seldom report when ex-convicts learn their lesson and return to a normal life, but an ex-convict who commits new crimes is more likely to make the news.

Unwed teenage mothers present a particularly poignant example of stigmatic harm. Sometimes little more than children themselves, they often possess only the vaguest idea of what it means to be an adult, much less a parent, and to exercise mature moral agency. But their irresponsible conduct—and especially that of the usually much older men who fathered and then abandoned their children—must be firmly condemned because of the immense harm that it will likely cause to themselves, their children, other teens who follow their example, and society more generally. Such condemnation is bound to stigmatize them, and if the stigma has the effect of reducing the number of other teenagers who have children out of wedlock, then the stigma will be socially salutary on balance, even if it seems unfair in particular cases. But voters may think of these teenage unwed parents, rightly or wrongly, as iconic representatives of a much broader group of recipients who upon greater reflection could be regarded as more deserving—for example, women who waited to have a child until they had the appropriate resources and maturity but who then lost a job or a husband. If voters frequently ascribe the first group's irresponsibility to the second, more deserving group, then the stigma of the first may attach to the second, with the political result being that the benefits of the latter group may be cut.[10] This unfavorable effect, which we call a *negative reputational externality*, indirectly harms good apple recipients.

When policymakers decide how to allocate resources, of course, they must consider a variety of factors, including reputational externalities, that cut in different directions: the potential to deter similar bad choices by other teenagers, the effects that withholding resources would have on the teenage parent's innocent children and on the teenager's own opportunities in the future, any unfairness in treating them categorically rather than as individuals, and so forth. Needless to say, these policy judgments are very difficult and must rest in part on fine legal and moral distinctions that political rhetoric tends to distort and obscure.

The stigma factor complicates the definition, analysis, and classification of bad apples. Stigma is a social construct; indeed, it may sometimes apply to individuals whose behavior is more morally praiseworthy, yet is also more legally culpable, than that of the teenage unwed parent. A particularly compelling example is the estimated 11 million undocumented immigrants in the United States. They are not immoral in any obvious sense. Indeed, many Americans (including us) admire those who work hard, albeit illegally, to support their families under the most difficult conditions. Like many other Americans, we imagine that we would behave the same were we in their straitened positions, and we recognize them as members of our communities for most purposes. Even so, they bear some similarities to bad apples. They knowingly violate the law, take resources away from citizens and legal immigrants, and often stigmatize those immigrants who hold legal status but who are erroneously lumped together with them by the public and sometimes law enforcement officers.[11] Their queue-jumping is unfair and harmful to good apple immigrants who wait for their green cards patiently and often at considerable personal cost, and it makes playing by the rules of the immigration system seem like a sucker's game. This in turn encourages many of those waiting in the queue to abandon it and instead try to enter illegally. In this way, the problem escalates.

We have no simple and satisfying answers to the very important question of how policymakers should deal with low-income unwed parents, illegal immigrants, and other groups whose behavior society wants—but has failed—to deter. Precisely because of the moral ambiguities surrounding these groups—concerns about the innocent children of these parents, and about the lack of legal status for these immigrants—the social costs of excluding them from social programs or legal status may be much higher than it is in the case of bad apples proper. Our purpose here is not to solve such policy problems but rather to help clarify how policymakers should analyze them with respect to how these groups affect good apples.

Resource Drains

Some individuals use program resources to an extent that is vastly disproportionate to the resources used by other recipients and perhaps also to their moral claims on the resources consumed. Examples include the frequently readmitted hospital patients, often serial substance abusers, who account for a remarkably high share of total hospital costs; patients who are on life support in a vegetative state for long periods of time; recidivist criminals; long-term welfare recipients (before the 1996 reform); and the chronically unemployed.[12] Although some resource drains are bad apples (for example, criminals) or bad bets (for example, vegetative patients), many resource drains are good apples. Indeed, some individuals who were resource drains in the past may even be good bets looking forward—a chronic drug abuser who is likely to abandon his habit because of an innovative rehabilitation program—though their extremely high costs and propensity to recidivism make this less likely. Despite the importance of resource drains to program budgets, we shall discuss such individuals only if they are also bad bets or bad apples. That is because individuals who are resource drains do not neatly fall into the bad bet or bad apple categories that are our chief interest and because those who are good apples and good bets are not the subject of our analysis.

Potential Overlap of Bad Bet and Bad Apple Categories in Individuals

Some individuals are unambiguously good bets and good apples. An example is the highly motivated, promising student awarded a need-based scholarship to college. But when it comes to bad bets and bad apples, there are almost always degrees of badness. Thus, the individual who will benefit only slightly from an expensive operation or the student who only disrupts occasionally might be thought of as semi-bad. In addition, many individuals will fall to some extent in both categories—for example, a substance abuser who has induced others to join him in dropping out of job training programs or a disruptive public housing tenant who has been using the apartment for drug transactions more than for shelter.

Analytically, the bad bet and bad apple categories are completely distinct. In reality, however, we expect that on average bad apples will be worse bets than other recipients—that is, bad apples will benefit less from the social programs that they spoil. Disrupting a program or engaging in activities that divert others—exemplars of bad apple behavior—are the types of actions that not only limit the bad apple's benefits but also reduce the benefits of others. Policymakers wishing to compute accurately the net benefits that good apples gain from their participation in a program must subtract these benefit reductions.

Figure 2-1 illustrates the possible combinations of status as a bad bet and bad apple. It shows where different individuals might fall on a scale from 0 to 1 in both the bad bet and bad apple categories, where a high score is good. Although our discussion in later chapters is divided between bad bets (chapter 4) and bad apples (chapter 5), the reader should recognize that many potential program beneficiaries exhibit elements of both.

We stress two propositions, implicit in the figure. Good and bad bets and good and bad apples are not discrete categories but fall along continua—even

Figure 2-1. *Ratings of Potential Recipients as Bets and Apples*

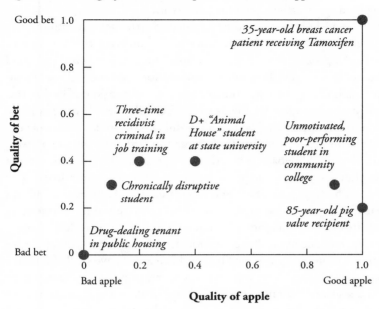

though we shall sometimes refer to them in discrete terms for simplicity's sake. Both categories count when determining which individuals merit assistance. Thus, someone who is a slightly bad bet but a very good apple should get services ahead of someone who is more of a bad bet but also a fairly bad apple. This figure moves us to the next critical question. Given that we know how individuals are classified, should they receive services? Because this is a central question for target efficiency, we discuss it through the remainder of the volume.

Bad bets and bad apples present two different answers. Bad apples are denied services primarily because they drain benefits from others. The wealth of a society or the size of its budget for social programs will generally not affect the judgment about whether a disruptive student's behavior is harmful enough to justify removal to another program. This decision will turn largely on the harm that he inflicts on the other students. Bad bets are different in this respect; society will want to prioritize them, and its wealth and budget for social programs will determine the cutoff point for deciding when a particular bet is to be deemed bad. Society will start by giving resources to those who will benefit most and will continue to do so until the budget that taxpayers provide is exhausted. In other words, societies with larger program budgets will proceed further down the priority list.

The type of analysis that would be required to systematically improve target efficiency is shown in figure 2-1, which locates different combinations of individuals and programs (treatments) on the good bet–bad bet and good apple–bad apple continua. Tamoxifen treatment for a 35-year-old breast cancer patient represents an excellent outcome on both dimensions. The 85-year-old recipient of a pig valve for the heart is an excellent apple but poor bet. The three-time recidivist criminal in a job training program is a bad apple but a so-so bet. This graph is meant to illustrate our thinking and be a visual metaphor. One could debate at length the appropriate location for each of these cases, but prioritization requires such ratings (or their equivalent). Note that we have arbitrarily scaled each of the axes from 0 to 1, where 0 is bad and 1 is good. There need be no cardinal meaning to these numbers so long as higher is better and the decisionmaker understands the rating scale.

The reader will encounter these individuals again, and many others, as we proceed through our analysis of bad bets and bad apples. We shall also return to figure 2-1 in chapter 7, where we add societal preferences—what some might call a social welfare function. This helps us draw together the lessons of this volume and to discuss in broad terms the nature of good and bad policies.

The Challenge of Employing the Definitions

Any particular definition of bad bets or bad apples will be highly contestable, as well it should be. Society must necessarily make highly controversial moral judgments. In addition, it can distinguish bad bets from good ones only by analyzing social costs and benefits. This in turn requires empirical determinations that for familiar reasons may be elusive and will surely be politicized, as in the case of organ allocation (see chapter 4).

Even if we could define the bad and good apple categories uncontroversially, the task of screening and classifying particular individuals—something every social program must ultimately do—will remain contentious, raising difficult issues of procedural fairness and even constitutional rights. For example, the principles of due process and equal protection under the Constitution significantly constrain the power of officials to withdraw public benefits from statutorily eligible recipients or from beneficiaries who must be included on equal protection grounds.[13] Within these legal constraints, policymakers must decide which kinds of institutions and competencies—professional, bureaucratic, judicial, religious, or other—are best suited to make the factual and normative determinations on which such assignments ultimately depend. In chapter 3, we discuss the large fiscal, substantive, and political stakes involved in avoiding bad bets and removing bad apples. These stakes require classifications that make accurate predictions and procedures that society accepts as legally adequate and fair. We take up this challenge in chapter 6.

Target Efficiency and Fairness

We defined target efficiency in chapter 1. In this section, we discuss how we assess it and then explain why the pursuit of target efficiency reinforces fairness goals rather than compromising them. We analyze both of these subjects in much greater technical detail in chapter 6, where we also describe the procedural protections that should accompany any well-targeted program.

The Goal

Public policies in a liberal democracy like ours should promote the welfare of society. The principal ingredient of social welfare is the aggregated well-being of individuals.[14] All social policies must somehow balance the welfare of some groups against the welfare of others. Unfortunately, policymakers lack a neat measuring device that indicates how much benefit an individual would receive from a proposed policy. The problem, however, is not merely one of measurement. Philosophers and policy analysts vigorously debate which measures would be appropriate, even assuming that such measures were available. Some try to settle the issue by arguing that democratic processes legitimate whatever policies that public deliberation, elections, and legislative processes produce.

This solution, however, simply moves the difficulty back a step. The compassionate taxpayers who pay for social programs that target bad draws—and who also determine the outcomes of elections—want their taxes to go where they will do the most good and to those who will secure the greatest benefits. That is what target efficiency is all about. We assume that taxpayers want it even though they may sometimes be willing to incur even large inefficiencies to achieve—or at least signal their commitment to—their normative goals, including compassion and fairness. They are most likely to make this sacrifice if the total cost is not too high and if the symbolic value of the gesture is great. This doubtless explains why society devotes immense medical resources to separating the fortunately rare cases of twins conjoined at the head.

Voters want to know what proposed programs can accomplish, how much welfare the programs will provide to which beneficiaries, and at what cost. They can only get answers to these questions if the policymakers who design and administer social programs employ a benefit-cost or cost-effectiveness criterion to get the most bang for the buck. This is so, moreover, even when the language surrounding the programs is not couched in these terms but instead emphasizes nonefficiency goals and procedural safeguards.

What do we mean by greatest benefits? Let us first consider classification along the continuum from good to bad bet. We maintain that a simple benefit-cost test should be—and for taxpayers is—the principal criterion for allocating program benefits. Consider the simplest case, tallying benefits in monetary terms. An example of this would be training programs that are meant to increase earnings. If the same training program would add $20,000 to the first trainee's discounted lifetime earnings but only $2,000 to the second trainee's, then the first trainee would be a very good bet relative to the second. If the training cost $5,000, then the first should get the training and the second should not, other things being equal.

Suppose there is a particular allotment of money for this training, say $100,000. Then target efficiency would dictate giving the program to the twenty people who would benefit the most from the expenditure. This cost-effectiveness approach—maximize effectiveness for whatever resources are being used—is most valuable in the typical case of administratively fixed budgets, unlike a case in which the budget can be adjusted flexibly according to the levels of benefits being produced.[15]

The approach is similar with bad apples. Here, however, we must subtract the costs that they impose on good apples from the benefits that they, the bad apples, derive from the program. Thus, if a bad apple secured $7,000 of future earnings from the training program while cutting the benefits of each of the nineteen other recipients by $300, his net benefits should be computed as $7,000 − $5,700 (19 x $300) = $1,300. This would be the calculation most favorable to the bad apple. Given the costs that he imposes, we might decide to value his benefits far below those of other individuals and certainly far below the costs that he imposes on others. In short, we might wish to remove him from the program even if he could be served at no direct monetary cost.

Fairness

Our recommended pursuit of target efficiency will exclude from programs many individuals, both bad apples and bad bets, who are currently included. Although this will often raise fairness issues, we will show that target efficiency is complementary to fairness values, not contradictory to them.

Fairness seems less of a concern with bad apples because their removal from a program results from their own bad conduct. Since they are imposing costs on others, allocating resources to them entails an element of injustice, independent of the level of waste. That said, bad apples in one policy arena should not automatically be considered bad apples in another policy arena, unless they also behave badly in that second arena. For example, criminals do not forfeit the right to medical care, and disruptive students should be allowed to participate in neighborhood recreation programs if they are not disruptive there.

Occasionally, sound policy dictates targeting specific resources to bad apples, namely when doing so would create substantial social benefits for the resources expended. A policy of giving medical care to tubercular felons or free needles to chronic addicts to prevent them from infecting others probably satisfies a benefit-cost test. We include these bad apples in such programs as a way to protect good apples and other bad apples.

Screening for bad apples is sometimes too costly or too intrusive to be socially acceptable, as courts have ruled with respect to some drug searches. In addition, the moralizing politics and rhetoric that are so characteristic of programs emphasizing group need or desert sometimes serve, perhaps by design, to obscure or marginalize efficiency considerations. Nevertheless, efficiency—that is, maximizing social benefits per unit of cost, within whatever constraints society decides to impose—is a compelling normative criterion even when the policy's primary goal is redistribution, and even when some of those who are denied resources are otherwise deemed deserving. Indeed, efficiency may be especially valuable in redistributive programs, given that wasting resources desperately needed by the destitute is particularly objectionable.

For bad bets, the complementary relationship between target efficiency and fairness is less obvious and more debatable. Allocating scarce resources to bad bets rather than to good bets is wasteful and surely unfair, even when the bad bets are good apples: for example, spending hundreds of thousands of dollars on an exemplary citizen who is near death or providing an extremely expensive, cost-ineffective medicine to a patient when an inexpensive substitute will be 98 percent as effective. Those same resources could accomplish much more for other citizens who need medical care. (See chapter 4.)

Those who pay for benefits (call them payers) and those who receive them (recipients) share an interest in enabling the recipients to secure the greatest possible welfare gain for whatever resources the payers make available. This is true whether the payers' contributions take the form of voluntary donations or a legally mandated tax. Accordingly, when payers support a food stamp program for recipients rather than an increase in welfare benefits, we should assume that payers believe, at least implicitly and all things considered, that this is the best way to help the recipients. Such beliefs are usually fortified by political factors. For example, the dramatic growth of the food stamp program, discussed in chapter 3, reflects the political influence of agribusiness and food retailing interests, not just the shape of voter altruism. Similarly, the expansion of medical care for low-income, elderly, and certain disabled people reflects the interests of providers and product suppliers, not merely society's concerns about the medically indigent, the elderly, and the disabled.

When recipients fall into distinct subgroups, payers face a challenging two-part task. Given a fixed sum for redistribution, should more go to group A or to group B? And if the program tilts towards the latter (say, because they are sicker than group A and can benefit more from medical resources), how should the program be designed to ensure this outcome? When some in group A are bad apples or bad bets but few or none in group B are, our analysis points to allocating a larger share of the available resources to group B, or perhaps all to group B and nothing to group A. Both compassion and efficiency values dictate that spending more on bad bets and bad apples is ordinarily unwise, irresponsible, and (in the case of bad apples) unjust.

Voters' Knowledge and Preferences

Voters do not make their social policy choices behind a Rawlsian veil of ignorance that conceals their future status or the resources they would receive under alternative policies.[16] Rather, they already know whether they are more or less likely to benefit from particular policy proposals—that is, whether they have already turned out to be good draws or bad draws. Suburbanites know that their own children and their neighbors' children are unlikely to suffer from failing inner-city schools, and college graduates do not anticipate having to rely on Medicaid.[17] To be sure, as discussed below, voters are public-spirited under certain common conditions, which a healthy polity will nurture. Nevertheless, we assume that they will usually base their votes on a proposal's perceived benefits and costs to them, which include whatever benefits they may enjoy from helping others. Voters who already know that they are good draws are likely to favor less redistribution than voters behind a Rawlsian veil of ignorance, who recognize that they might turn out to be bad draws.

We would not expect to find such a difference in voters' perspectives, however, when they are allocating the same pot of resources between good and bad apples. Consider voters behind the veil to whom only one piece of information is revealed: they are told whether or not they will be parents of schoolchildren. We believe that these two groups would make similar decisions about how to allocate resources between good and bad apple students, assuming that they knew that the disruptive ones would be placed in a separate school and that per pupil costs would remain the same. (In chapter 5, we discuss the possibility of separate programs for bad apples, including programs that could entail higher expenditures per pupil.) Parents would worry that their child might be a bad apple disrupter; they would also worry that their child would be a good apple whose education would be disrupted by bad apples. All voters would consider the relative effects of separating these two groups of students, and they presumably would roughly weigh them by the numbers in each category. Similarly, if forced to vote on allocations to the separate schools, not yet knowing whether their child would be disruptive, parents and committed nonparents with a civic stake in the issue should favor roughly equivalent per pupil allocations. For the same reason, these two groups are also likely to make the same decision about whether to separate the bad apples.

Despite substantial private charity—$289 billion in 2004, about 75 percent from individual donors—most of the resources redistributed to bad draws come from the state, and state policy tends to follow voters' preferences.[18] Voting for traditional social programs for the poor must be overwhelmingly altruistic. Most voters know that they are unlikely to need these programs themselves. Thus, for example, we see that voters support, through taxes and philanthropy, benefits for the victims of disasters, such as Hurricane Katrina, which they think or know they are most unlikely to experience themselves.[19]

To be sure, social programs that target the poor constitute a much smaller proportion of governmental transfers than those that mostly benefit the non-poor, such as Social Security, Medicare, and some tax expenditures such as the deductibility of home mortgage interest. But survey data and voting behavior clearly demonstrate that voters and elected officials strongly support social programs designed to assist those low-income Americans who voters think are down on their luck, cannot help themselves, and would work hard to improve their lot if capable of working and if given the chance.[20] Private giving to programs for the poor, which is overwhelmingly delivered through nonprofit organizations that target in their own way, provides further evidence of generosity in a broad-based public.

Nevertheless, voters' willingness to support programs that confer little or no benefit on themselves is limited, and they weigh the benefits going to program recipients as a function of the costs in higher taxes they themselves must bear. Voters will agree to redistribute resources (through government programs or private charity) only when they think that those who receive them will benefit more from those resources than would the taxpayers who would otherwise spend them in different ways. In addition, voters must be convinced that resources are not going to the wrong people. Voters are altruistic only up to a point. If they think that too many resources are going to bad apples or even to good apples who are bad bets, their limited altruism will be sorely tested and may cease altogether. We return to this point in chapter 5. (Voters' attitudes toward bad bets are also complicated, but for quite different reasons that are discussed in chapter 4.)

Needless to say, information about program effectiveness is not optimal, voters are not always rational, and the political rhetoric surrounding social programs is often designed—or in any event operates—to obscure this benefit-cost framework.[21] This rhetoric of justification, for example, may insist that assistance be given on the basis of a recipient's individual or group rights, to compensate for past injustices, to benefit a locality, or simply to help current unfortunates. In addition to these plausible and sometimes compelling justifications for redistribution, legislators may have self-interested reasons to support transfers quite apart from taxpayers' interests. For example, legislators may be beholden to groups that provide services to the beneficiaries or may wish to cultivate a reputation for compassion.

Typical voters cannot always identify situations with too many bad bets or even bad apples as readily as a policy specialist could, but they may learn about such situations through public discussion, government or media reports, or their own experiences with or observations of program participants. In addition, the program's opponents will strive to draw their attention to the existence of bad apples and bad bets. Past demands for reform of the welfare system, Medicaid, the Earned Income Tax Credit (EITC), food stamps, and student loan programs exemplify voters' impatience with poorly targeted programs. Politicians both reflect this impatience and exploit it for their own electoral or ideological advantage.

Note that in this discussion we have defined bad draws in conventional terms; they are individuals whose misfortune is not a result of their bad choices. Despite their misfortune, society might still want to give them less than they need as defined by some objective measure. Individuals making decisions behind the Rawlsian veil of ignorance (at least if they embrace our social welfare criterion) should want to allocate resources so that the welfare gained from an additional dollar spent would be the same across all social programs. If policymakers allocated funds in this way, then needier claimants in a particular program would receive more resources than would better-off participants in that or perhaps any program. However, needier claimants still may not receive enough to alleviate all of what some would define as their need. Attaining that standard could be too costly in relation to either the benefits produced or the benefits possible through alternative allocations.

Here, "too costly" is judged by voters and politicians—not by the recipients, their advocates, or program administrators.

Rationing

In a world of limited resources, the importance of target efficiency lends urgency to the inevitable need to prioritize among social welfare expenditures. This urgency is perhaps most apparent in programs subsidizing medical care. Such prioritizing—often a euphemism for the dread word rationing—is now common, though most often concealed or inadvertent, and will become more common in the future.[22]

Public and political resistance to this prioritizing is greatest when the losers under such systems—the elderly and severely ill, for example—are readily identifiable. In chapter 4, we discuss the resistance that rationing efforts met, and succumbed to, in Oregon and the United Kingdom. In contrast, managed care organizations that are less politically constrained routinely place roadblocks in the way of expensive procedures that they think will yield relatively few benefits for the resources used—rationing practices that are almost certain to become even more common.[23] As any doctor can attest, many other formal and informal rationing methods are employed, even as those doing the rationing may deny this fact.

Rationing, of course, is extremely controversial, and even the most sophisticated policy analysts may shrink from discussing it. For example, in reviewing a book about rationing, Paul Krugman and Robin Wells maintain that policymakers should not address rationing unless and until they make the current system more efficient.[24] But there is every reason to do both. Policymakers should increase productive efficiency *and* consider the soundest approaches to targeting, including rationing services, rather than merely entertain the vain hope that new efficiencies will somehow turn up and obviate the need for rationing. Even in the unlikely event that we could eliminate all inefficiencies, there would be no good reason to waste resources by spending them where they will accomplish little.

Even where policymakers accept the need for rationing and its allocative and political consequences, contentious methodological, empirical, and normative issues remain. The Environmental Protection Agency, for example, has been debating the particular method by which its policies should be assessed and prioritized.[25] Whatever the relative merits of particular ranking methods, we maintain that a compassionate society should generally prioritize its expenditures with a view to maximizing the social benefits generated and that this principle should not be confined to health-related issues. To illustrate, for any given overall expenditure on poverty-assistance programs, social welfare would be increased if we could make consistent and accurate tradeoffs among the social benefits of cash transfers, health services, education, and other ameliorative policies. Giving a poor person $1,000 in cash may benefit him more than spending $1,000 on his health care. If so, and if this choice has no other undesirable effects, target efficiency would dictate giving him the cash.

Regardless of how policymakers rank and compute benefits, they must still prioritize their expenditures. As we explain in chapters 4 and 5, this precept has far-reaching implications for the substantial resources that now flow as cash or to support services for bad bets and bad apples.

After Bad Bets Are Avoided and Bad Apples Are Removed

Efficiency and equity are the main themes in this book. Under the bad bets analysis, society should avoid investing resources where they will accomplish little if anything. We do not see this as a troubling issue of equity because we think all taxpayers would agree to such a principle behind a veil of ignorance.

But what should happen to the bad bets: the 90-year-old who does not get a heart valve transplant or the student with little chance of passing who is not admitted to a community college? The 90-year-old should receive less invasive and less expensive medical treatment. The student should receive the option of vocational training, which probably would add more to his or her future income and self-image than would enrolling in and then dropping out of college. And if the student's academic potential improves, then he or she should also be able to gain admission to the community college.

Deciding what to do with bad apples once they are removed presents a much harder challenge. Laws often give them a right to certain publicly subsidized services. In New York City, the homeless are entitled to shelter even if they misbehave. A highly disruptive 16-year-old is still entitled to attend school, and sound social policy would probably send this student to some school even if it were not required. Our first priority, however, is to protect the good apples whose educational opportunities would be spoiled by bad apples in their midst. This choice implies that the disruptive student should be placed in an alternative program. If the student's disruptive conduct continues, other bad apples in that program will be harmed. They also deserve protection, but less so than the good apples back in the original school. It is likely, however, that the disruptive student will cause less harm in the alternative program. If that program is well designed and the student's conduct improves, then a return to the original program may be appropriate.

New York City's public shelters, as we shall see in chapter 5, sometimes remove bad apple families from their ranks and place them in private housing. Shelter officials believe that simply throwing these families out on the street is neither legal (they are entitled to shelter at public expense), fair (some family members may be good apples), nor cost-effective (they will continue to harm others and themselves). These officials, however, are often willing to pay a high premium just to get these bad apples off their hands. This pattern is by no means confined to New York City.[26] Needless to say, such perverse incentives, if widely employed and understood, would not only be very costly but at the margin would induce some good apples to engage in sufficiently bad behavior to get "punished" by being placed in superior housing. Such behavior is much in the spirit of students (or their parents) exaggerating learning disorders in order to secure individual tutoring, more time on exams, or other advantages.

Were bad apples evicted from public housing—as distinguished from shelters, the housing of last resort that cannot be denied—they would be no worse off than the vast majority of poor people whose low income makes them eligible for a unit but who do not receive one. They would lose a subsidy that is given to a small percentage of poor people but denied to all the others. This hardly seems unfair or inequitable. If the bad apples' behavior is sufficiently bad, they may be left to their fate in the market. Alternatively, they may be placed in heavily supervised halfway houses with others who misbehave.

The examples of the high school, shelter, and public housing bad apples illustrate an important principle. After bad apples are removed from programs intended for good ones, many of them are, alas, likely to remain bad apples. Anticipating this, program administrators should determine which kind of placement will be a good bet for the removed bad apple. Sometimes, however, no program will be a good bet for these people. In that case, letting them fend for themselves may be the least bad choice among a poor set of options, one whose chief virtue is that the bad apples will no longer be in a position to diminish the welfare of good apples or to consume public subsidies yielding a low or even negative payoff.

Society does provide programs that it thinks would be more beneficial to recidivist criminals, high school bullies, shelter abusers, and public housing disrupters than would leaving these people in situations that might enable or encourage them to harm others. Any resulting reduction in the harm that these miscreants can inflict should be counted as a benefit. If these programs for bad apples cost more than the counterpart programs for good apples, the excess costs may still be acceptable if the removal notably improves the lot of good apples in aggregate.

Although avoiding bad bets by definition saves social resources that can then be used to better effect in other ways, removing bad apples may not have this resource effect. Indeed, it is possible that transferring them to alternative programs may end up costing society as much or more in purely fiscal terms than leaving them in mainstream programs. We lack the data to assess this possibility (although not for want of trying).[27] The principal justification for removal—the protection of good apples and their opportunities to advance—is moral, not fiscal.

3

High Stakes, Misguided Evasions, and Bad Policies

This chapter consists of three parts. First, we describe the stakes involved in improving target efficiency in social programs, with a focus on the importance of avoiding bad bets and removing bad apples. Second, we consider certain recurring impediments to reform and the failure of politicians, bureaucrats, and well-targeted redistributionists to take on the problems created by bad bets and bad apples. Given the high stakes, this failure represents a significant missed opportunity to increase support for programs designed to help bad draws who are good apples. Third, we offer a taxonomy of bad policy types. Here, we distinguish between policy types that are bad primarily because they represent poor targeting and those types that are bad for other reasons. As to the former, we identify six common "pathologies" that reduce target efficiency across a wide range of existing programs. These pathologies, we predict, will persist unless policymakers adopt the approach urged in this book.

The Social Policy Stakes

Bad apples and bad bets impose fiscal costs, substantive policy costs, and political costs on society. However, bad bets and bad apples impose these three kinds of burdens quite differently. The fiscal stakes in avoiding bad bets are much higher than they are with bad apples, but the substantive policy and political costs created by bad apples have little application to bad bets.

Fiscal Costs

Resources available for social programs are always limited relative to the demands made on them, but rarely more so than today. Although our economy is now much larger than it was when most of these programs were established, the claims against those resources have grown even more. The federal government is now running the highest deficit ever in absolute terms, one that is widely viewed as unsustainable. The deficit as a percentage of GDP is not as high as it was in the mid-1980s. However, from 2003 to 2005, it represented a larger share of GDP than it did at any time in the last decade.[1] The two largest expenditure categories in the federal budget—Social Security and defense—are growing rapidly and will increase sharply in the future. The Social Security (Old-Age and Survivors Insurance and Disability Insurance) Trust Funds, though now in surplus, are projected to turn to deficit roughly around 2018 and to be exhausted in 2040.[2] Both parties acknowledge that the government must soon shore them up with some combination of additional revenues from taxes and contributions and benefit reductions, although they disagree about the appropriate mix of these measures. Military expenditures, which declined significantly as a percentage of the budget during the 1990s, are expanding because of the demands of technological change, higher force levels, enhanced recruitment incentives, open-ended wars in Afghanistan and particularly in Iraq, growing global instability, inadequate military spending by America's allies, and the threat of terrorism. In addition, both political parties are committed to substantially increased federal expenditures on health care for an aging population.

The Medicare deficit, though attracting little attention, looms large. It is projected to swamp the Social Security deficit, and the hospital insurance trust fund is expected to run out of money in 2018, two years earlier than the estimate made only a year before.[3] The elderly demand many of the costly technologies and new products and services that are flooding the medical marketplace. The 2003 amendments to Medicare that created a new drug benefit for the elderly are just the beginning. Further in the medical arena, one can predict expanded care for children who are still not covered by Medicaid despite several previous program expansions, as the federal government moves in piecemeal fashion to reduce the size of the large and growing uninsured population. (At the same time, some states are expanding their own health insurance programs within the serious constraints imposed by their fiscal constitutions and conditions.)[4]

Yet neither party seems willing to support higher taxes to pay for this great range of endeavors. The Bush administration seeks to make its earlier tax cuts permanent and even increase them in certain areas such as Health Savings Accounts, while the 2004 Democratic platform proposed only to restore the pre-Bush tax rates on those earning more than $200,000, a measure that would curb but not end the deficit. Given these fiscal constraints, public expectations, and political commitments, the only good way to stretch programmatic resources is to target benefits more on those who can make the best use of them and who most deserve the public's solicitude and support. This means substantially excluding bad apples and avoiding bad bets.

Two commonly mentioned ways (other than improving administrative efficiency) to increase social benefits under these fiscal constraints deserve brief mention. The first, attacking fraud and abuse in public programs, is always popular. Every administration promises to achieve it. Like everyone else, we favor this strategy. But as explained in chapter 5, the kinds of bad apples who are of chief concern in this book, and especially worrisome, are those who are not engaged in fraud and abuse but who instead are eligible program participants. The second alternative, shifting the costs of public policies to the private sector through regulatory mandates, changes the initial cost-bearer but does not necessarily effect a more efficient and fairer distribution of the benefits, much less expand those benefits. If effective resource allocation and fair distribution are the policy goals, regulatory mandates may be little more than sleights of hand.

Absent active reform measures, we anticipate that the incidence of bad apples and bad bets in social programs will grow. Consider bad apples first. Their incentive to exploit the program benefits that they receive—public housing or schooling, for example—remains strong and tends to increase over time as they gain skill in doing so.[5] In addition, growing budget stringency often means—foolishly to be sure—that fewer resources will be devoted to monitoring and sanctioning bad apples. In recent years, the Internal Revenue Service (IRS)—for some combination of budgetary and political reasons—has reduced the number of taxpayer audits it conducts. This has almost certainly increased the incidence of intentional underpayments and outright fraud by bad apple taxpayers and thereby *increased* the deficit. Between 1996 and 2001, the number of apparent nonfilers increased about three and one-half times faster than the tax-filing population. Likewise, underreporting increased about one and one-half times faster.

Indeed, the IRS seems to be pursuing the worst-off taxpayers, since most of those in poverty do not pay income taxes at all, and its auditing program disproportionately targets the working poor, who are about eight times more likely to be audited than are investment partnerships.[6] This IRS practice primarily reflects increased enforcement efforts directed at fraudulent applications for the Earned Income Tax Credit (EITC), yet the estimated tax revenue that is lost to cheating on capital gains is more than four times the highest estimate cited by Congress for revenue losses in the EITC. In fact, the National Taxpayer Advocate has shown that most of these losses are not related to cheating.[7] The sharp reduction in interior enforcement, especially in workplaces, by the Bureau of Immigration and Customs Enforcement in the Department of Homeland Security, represents another example of this reduced deterrence (albeit one not involving bad apples as we have defined them). Undocumented workers who manage to make it into the country, or those workers who overstay their visas, face a very low risk of detection, much less removal; similarly, their employers are unlikely to be sanctioned for continuing to employ them.[8]

Several developments foreshadow an even faster rate of increase in bad bets compared with the rate of increase of bad apples. First is the extraordinary growth and improvement in medical technology, products, and services and the expansion in subsidized health insurance (including Medicare, Medicaid, veterans programs, civil service benefit programs, and tax expenditures for health insurance premiums) to cover increased medical expenditures.[9] This vast expansion in health care subsidies is bound to increase the number and the average cost of bad bets treated in the system.

Increased vulnerability to moral hazard—the propensity to take on more risk when one knows that others (here, a public program) will bear much of the expected cost of that risk—is a second reason to expect a continuing growth in bad bets. Most social programs adopted during the New Deal era were designed (sometimes inadvertently) to minimize moral hazard by targeting individuals whose misfortunes occurred through no fault of their own. Since these misfortunes were common, the risks of such losses could be reduced or socialized by being spread among a much larger pool of individuals. Programs of this kind, and many others as well, are like insurance contracts in which one does not know ex ante which individuals will be sick and which ones will stay healthy, which ones will be disabled and which remain able-bodied, which ones will be laid off and which employed, and so forth. These features help to justify the transfer of resources to those unfortunates who turn out to be bad draws. They also make the programs, once they mature, actuarially feasible. A rational and risk-averse citizen behind the Rawlsian veil of ignorance would presumably favor such a system.

Not all social programs create moral hazard. For example, benefits for the elderly, widows, wounded war veterans, and the seriously disabled entail little or no moral hazard, either because the beneficiaries have no way to affect either the likelihood or the magnitude of the compensable event (old age, spousal death) or because the compensable event (serious disability) is so debilitating that no one would willingly incur it. But many policies of recent decades do engender additional moral hazard—and thus create more bad bets. For example, the availability of unemployment insurance on relatively easy terms often encourages individuals to refuse to seek or take a new job until their benefits run out, particularly in areas where jobs are plentiful.[10] Similarly, workers' compensation programs have long been plagued by easy-to-claim and hard-to-disprove complaints of back pain.[11] Health insurance may also create moral hazard by reducing the costs of self-destructive behavior. Examples include publicly subsidized coverage of costly treatments for emphysema (which is almost always caused by smoking) or of organ transplants for heavy drinkers. If the moral hazard in such programs becomes too great, these bad bets may become bad apples, demoralizing and stigmatizing the good apples who surround them.

When policies create entitlements for which broadly defined groups of individuals are categorically eligible, such policies virtually ensure that more of the program's resources will go to bad bets.[12] In addition to entitlements, other broad benefit expansions can increase moral hazard, particularly when the criteria for denying or limiting benefits are more difficult to define and apply, as they are with mental health. For example, the adoption in 1996 of the Mental Health Parity Act, which requires insurance coverage for federally funded mental health services to be comparable with that for physical health services, prompted a flurry of similar state legislation. As of May 2000, thirty-one states had such laws.[13] The Medicare Prescription Drug Improvement and Modernization Act of 2003, which provides a prescription drug benefit for seniors (Part D), represents an even more dramatic expansion of programmatic moral hazard by inducing excess use of low-benefit drugs.[14] As a final example of moral hazard encouraging bad bets, the many state laws requiring health insurance plans to cover medical treatments for diabetes may have the perverse effect of displacing individuals' behavioral precautions, which are essential to successful diabetes management.[15]

Social programs creating personal moral hazard are dwarfed by those involving commercial moral hazard, such as federal insurance programs on savings deposits, pensions, and mortgages.[16] Much the same is true of the massive subsidies to individuals, businesses, and communities in the wake of natural disasters, such as Hurricane Katrina, which create powerful incentives to relocate and rebuild in notoriously vulnerable areas.[17] Drought insurance programs in the western part of the country have analogous undesirable effects. They encourage overdevelopment in arid regions that in turn requires more insurance and more water projects. Bad bets are attracted to such programs and are often common within them.

One prominent expert on social insurance, Jerry Mashaw, takes a quite different view on moral hazard. He argues that "virtually every income support program, from pensions to the EITC, is constructed with elaborate attention to moral hazard issues. . . ." He notes that vocational rehabilitation and other service programs have elaborate restrictions on overserving bad bets and that "Medicare spending on catastrophic care has caps, and nursing home care is restricted to 3 months."[18] Accepting such examples, we think that Mashaw underestimates the magnitude of the moral hazard problem. One cannot adopt broad-based provisions, such as mandated parity for mental health insurance and Medicare drug benefits, without increasing moral hazard. Neither patient nor doctor has the incentive to restrict services to situations of high cost-effectiveness. In the case of Medicare, most of the bad bets in the program are not the few people who run up against programmatic limits but the multitude who receive treatments and procedures that are expensive yet offer few benefits. The expense is usually in medical resources, although sometimes an irreplaceable scarce resource is involved, such as a cadaver kidney, which compounds the loss from poor targeting.

We do not mean to suggest that the moral hazard issue is decisive in deciding how to design most social programs. Nevertheless, it is a very important factor, which we discuss at greater length in the chapters that follow.

Substantive Policy Costs

Although bad apples and bad bets both waste scarce program resources, bad apples undermine a program's substantive policy goals in other ways, which we discuss in chapter 5. There, we explain how bad apples directly hurt good apples and also impose indirect harms on them and on others. We also present data on particularly troubling, widespread, and persistent examples in three kinds of social programs: chronically disruptive public school students who interfere with the learning opportunities of their already deprived classmates; chronically disruptive public housing residents who impair their neighbors' quality of life; and residents of homeless shelters whose rule-breaking make difficult living conditions in the shelters significantly worse.

Political Costs

Misallocating program resources to bad apples and bad bets squanders the political capital needed to sustain programs for good apples and good bets. Misallocation provides powerful political ammunition to a program's enemies while weakening support among its friends. (As we explain at the end of this chapter, however, the effects of misallocation on bad bets are not identical to the effects on bad apples.)

If voters' altruism is indeed limited, as suggested in chapter 2, then programs that effectively screen out or remove bad apples will tend to increase their political legitimacy, which in turn can enhance their long-run public support and even increase their funding (at least by making more funds available per good apple). Voters and legislators may not know how many bad apples a program contains and may accept that a few in a program are probably inevitable. However, they can more readily distinguish between programs that earnestly strive to weed out bad apples and those that do not, and they will give more support to those programs that make a strong effort to do so while withdrawing support from those that do not. Leading examples of this effect of improved targeting on public support are the 1996 welfare reform law, the Earned Income Tax Credit, and the Food Stamp program. We also discuss this effect in chapter 5.

The Personal Responsibility and Work Opportunity Reconciliation Act (PRWORA), passed by Congress in 1996, imposed a stiff work requirement designed to prevent welfare recipients who are deemed capable of work from remaining on the rolls indefinitely (which would make them bad apples).[19] The new program (Temporary Assistance for Needy Families [TANF]) maintained federal funding at the pre-reform level in nominal terms, when one includes the additional funds that were appropriated for child care and other work support services. Because the number of those who remained on the rolls (relatively good apples) was much lower, TANF and these other work support programs produced significantly increased funding to aid good apple working poor families.[20] This development continued even after the election of a much more conservative president and a somewhat more Republican Congress. Subsidies to low-income families for child care provided outside TANF, but directly related to TANF's goal of work promotion, also increased substantially after welfare reform, as did funding for job training.[21] Congress provided these additional funds with the hope and expectation that welfare reform would enable wage incomes to replace transfer payments. Another provision of the reform, which limited noncitizens' access to federally funded public benefits, has had a similar political effect, weakening an argument—

immigrant dependency on welfare—that restrictionists traditionally used to press for lower immigration to the United States.[22]

The Earned Income Tax Credit (a federal transfer program that augments the income of low-wage working people) provides a further example of reform in a desirable direction. Since 1988, Congress and the IRS have taken steps to reduce fraud and other kinds of noncompliance with program requirements, although many such problems continue. For example, an IRS study of tax year 1994 found that 26 percent of dollars were overclaimed, down from 35 percent in 1988.[23] Reforms were designed to remove bad apples from the EITC program and to stem the loss of political support suffered by the pre-reform program. Significant problems of over- and underpayment certainly remain; the most recent estimates are that between 23 percent and 28 percent of EITC claims (between $9.8 billion and $11.6 billion) were erroneously paid on 2005 returns. Even so, the reformers' strategy seems to have succeeded in increasing congressional confidence in the program, as measured by a more than doubling of the real dollar value of EITC benefits.[24] This crackdown on fraud and overpayments, however, seems to have had several perverse effects. First, it has produced more complex EITC eligibility rules, which confuse claimants and tax preparation services and thus increase the error rate. These errors in turn are widely portrayed as fraud rather than innocent mistakes. Second, the crackdown has increased *under*-payments, a significant problem of a different kind, which is exacerbated by the lack of any agency incentive to avoid such underpayments.[25] As explained in chapter 6, agency incentives affect the frequency of certain kinds of administrative errors.

The Food Stamp program offers a third example of how reforms that improve targeting to remove bad apples can increase benefits to the remaining good apples. As with the EITC program, fraud and abuse of the Food Stamp program aroused much public indignation. In one respect, indignation about food stamps was even greater than that directed at other social programs. According to David Super, a close analyst of the program, "Middle-income voters could not tell whether a dollar they saw spent in the store originally came from an AFDC check, but they could see food stamps being transacted and often felt an impulse to pass judgment on recipients' purchases. Perhaps as a result, some polls found that the public classified food stamps as 'welfare' more often than it did AFDC."[26] Yet the program's advocates managed to reform it operationally and politically, increasing both federal and state financial support for the program. They did so, in part, by switching to electronic benefit transfer, which gave the public more confidence that benefits were being more closely monitored for fraud. In other ways, the program was redesigned to emphasize assistance to good apples in the working poor population, while making it harder for bad apples to remain eligible.[27] In New York City, Mayor Michael Bloomberg even over-ruled his top social service officials and conspicuously insisted that the city not pursue a federal waiver that would have made it easier for unemployed but able-bodied, childless adults to receive food stamps.[28] As with welfare and the EITC, congressional criticism of the food stamp program is less prominent today than it was a decade ago before the reforms removed some bad apples, added many good apples (the working poor), and made other changes unrelated to the bad apples issue.[29]

Sometimes the political linkage between reforms that remove bad apples and more resources for good apples can be inferred even when it is not explicit. Christopher Jencks, a leading sociologist who specializes in research on poverty and social programs, points out that the Clinton administration's welfare policymakers thought that they needed to expand the EITC program before they attempted welfare reform because they had to convince them-selves and those to their left that single mothers with minimum wages could make it.[30] Congress also raised the minimum wage within days of passing welfare reform, despite the hostility of the House leadership under Newt Gingrich to such proposals, and the states that reduced the number of wel-fare beneficiaries on their rolls spent a lot of money on child care subsidies and other job supports, including, in some cases, more generous increases of the EITC. A recent report suggests that they are continuing to do so: "States have poured money into education, training and child care to help welfare recipients get and keep jobs. Forty-four states said they would maintain cash assistance benefits in 2005 at the levels in effect this year. Five states . . . said they planned to increase cash assistance benefits next year."[31] Spending on child care subsidies, which enabled former recipients to work, almost dou-bled between the enactment of welfare reform and 2003, although working poor families in some states have had difficulty accessing these funds.[32]

When asked whether the reforms removing bad apples contributed signifi-cantly to such policy responses, Jencks replied, "I'd say yes, but the case is cir-cumstantial."[33] Originally an opponent of the welfare reform legislation, he now believes that

> the people who claimed that [the 1996 law] would cause a lot of suffer-ing no longer have much credibility with middle-of-the-road legisla-tors, who see welfare reform as an extraordinary success. If we want to regain credibility, we need to admit that welfare reform turned out so much better than we expected, and figure out why that was the case.

The usual explanation is just that the economy did better than anyone projected, but that is only part of the story.[34] A government social program whose performance exceeds expectations is a "man bites dog" story, one that merits close attention and investigation.[35]

To test our claim that removing bad apples from social programs for the poor can reduce the stigma associated with those programs, we investigated how often the epithet "welfare fraud" appeared in the *New York Times* between 1990 and 2005. A few states received waivers from federal welfare restrictions and initiated reforms starting in July 1992,[36] but the passage of PRWORA in August 1996 was the pivotal event. The results show a dramatic increase in the use of the term in the years leading up to the 1996 law and a sharp decline thereafter, with only 8 uses in 2005 compared with 67 in 1995.[37] Indeed, the most remarkable result is that welfare as a subject for news stories also decreased dramatically. The term "welfare recipient" was used in 482 stories in 1997, and the number since then has steadily fallen to only 30 stories in 2005. (See figure 3-1, which shows the frequency with which both "welfare fraud" and "welfare recipient" were used.) For those on welfare, the best discussion is no discussion; after all, most attention has been negative. Welfare reform evidently greatly reduced the media attention paid to welfare recipients, presumably in part because politicians made fewer efforts to stigmatize them, but the TANF block grant did not reduce total government expenditures on behalf of the poor—indeed, as we have seen, it freed up significant additional funds to aid the expanded group of working poor.

Some Perverse Impediments to Reform

The stakes in excluding bad apples from, and avoiding bad bets in, social programs are immense; they will only increase in the future. Why, then, is there so little enthusiasm for reforms?

There are several answers, some of them developed in Guido Calabresi and Philip Bobbitt's classic analysis of "tragic choices."[38] Perhaps the easiest explanation to understand is the universal psychosocial desire to affirm deeply held social values. In a world of scarce resources, policymakers must often publicly deny claims that seem morally compelling. So poignant are these choices and so eager are we to avoid moral responsibility for them that we contrive ways to disguise and obscure the choices, or at least conceal their tragic nature.

Sometimes we diffuse accountability for such choices by rendering them more anonymous or implicit and thus harder to identify and criticize. Some-

Figure 3-1. *Articles Mentioning "Welfare Recipient" and "Welfare Fraud" in the* New York Times, *1990–2005*

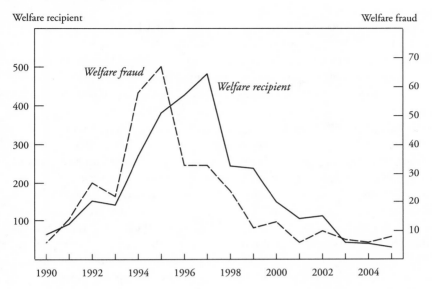

Welfare recipient

Welfare fraud

times we delegate the choices to opaque but legitimating processes, such as juries, ballot referenda, legal procedures, and other "black box" mechanisms that need not (and in some cases, may not) either explain or justify their decisions.[39] Mechanisms invoking random choice, such as lotteries; somewhat opaque processes, such as budget reconciliation bills; or relatively impersonal ones, such as markets, also provide little or no justifying information, though the outcomes of markets (unlike most random and opaque mechanisms) are seldom quirky.[40]

Legislatures, agencies, courts, and other governmental institutions that do give reasons for their actions often conceal their choices (and mistakes) in processes that are intricate, protracted, or disembodied. Thus subcommittee decisions and procedural votes play a major role in determining legislative outcomes. Whether deliberately or not, central elements of our constitutional and political system (such as separation of powers, federalism, localism, bicameral legislature, judicial review, interest group access to decisionmakers, administrative processes, and many more) effectively diffuse initiative, disguise responsibility, obscure exercises of power, and mask our collective tragic choices.

These institutional responses to the problem of tragic choices tend to enhance individual freedoms and exhibit other values favored by a liberal polity. At the same time, however, they often produce bad policies by rendering crucial facts more resistant to analysis. More to our point, these responses make it more likely that society will allocate too many resources to bad apples and bad bets rather than to other bad draws for whom the resources could bear more fruit. The opacity of these bad policies confounds rational voting and policymaking. It also makes it harder for the disadvantaged to mobilize politically and legally to secure remedies.

The dynamics of public choice provide another reason why policymakers do not focus more on bad apples and bad bets.[41] Generally speaking, bad bets harm two different kinds of groups, and bad apples harm a third. The first harmed group is composed of the disadvantaged good bets and good apples who might otherwise claim the resources now wasted on bad bets and bad apples. This group will usually be too anonymous, amorphous, and perhaps ignorant of this waste and its effect on them to assert such claims. These features of the group make it harder for it to mobilize and exert pressure on officials, which in turn makes it less likely that officials will try to reform these bad policies. The second harmed group is the taxpayers who fund the bad policies. Taxpayers too are diffuse and difficult to organize as such, but once aroused they are a group whom policymakers are eager to please.

The third group, harmed only by bad apples, is composed of the bad apples' identifiable victims, such as the students whose learning is disrupted, the families whose public housing is degraded, and the shelter dwellers who are placed at risk. At least in principle, these victims of bad apples—being together and on the scene—could protest, mobilize, and remedy their conditions by pressing for policy changes. In fact, these victims may be too poor, ill-informed, or otherwise politically disadvantaged to organize effectively on their own behalf. That bad policies often persist because most of their victims lack a unified, effective voice is hardly news to any student of politics and public policy.

The persistence of bad bets reflects a number of factors. Distinguishing between good bets and bad bets can be difficult, and we have seen that society will go to great lengths to obscure or even deny the existence of tragic choices. But when the bad bets are good apples, society is even less inclined to make these tragic choices explicit. It makes people uneasy, for example, to reflect that the benefits of many social policies tend to be greater for young people than they are for the elderly (if only because the young will live longer) and that this sometimes justifies allocating medical resources to the young for conditions less pressing than those for which old people would be denied. (Chapter 4 discusses this phenomenon in detail.) People may feel that silence on precisely these kinds of judgments is necessary to maintain the social solidarity of a healthy political community—even at some cost in mis-allocated resources. Or their silence may instead reflect a fear of being viewed as ageist, punitive, callous, or otherwise inhumane. (By a parity of reasoning, of course, their support for the status quo might cause them to fear being called antichild or anti–working family, as those groups receive fewer resources when the elderly receive more.) We prefer a more pragmatic approach. This silence might be acceptable if it provided considerable social comfort in exchange for a modest misallocation of resources. But in fact the silence protects little. Most voters, we think, have sufficient inkling about the bad bets problem to limit their altruism, whereas significant resources are misallocated by the policymakers' failure to avoid bad bets.

Turning to bad apples, the persistence of policy choices that benefit them at the expense of good apples is partly explained by the "see no evil, hear no evil, speak no evil" behavior of many of the very people who claim to be most solicitous of the good apples' welfare—and who should therefore be most eager to exclude recipients whose behavior harms them. Indeed, these solicitous citizens deplore such terms as "bad apple" or "undeserving"; they view these terms as moral or political provocations that are meant to distract us from the social disadvantages that bad draws suffer and that discredit, dis-serve, and disrespect bad draws.[42] They charge that those persons (like us) who call attention to the depredations of bad apples are in effect blaming the victim. Although this charge tends (and is sometimes intended) to stop the conversation, we stubbornly continue it in the final section of this chapter.

The kindest thing to be said about this "conspiracy of silence" concerning bad apples is that the conspirators mean well. As Christopher Jencks says, "Bad apples have always been the weak underbelly of liberal compassion, and also of the 'rights'-oriented approach to social policy. I suppose the clearest case is in dealing with crime, but there it almost goes without saying."[43] Many advocates for the poor believe that avoiding or changing the subject in this fashion does in fact help the poor, and they fear that support for social programs would erode if the bad apples problem were widely discussed. They may also reinforce, if not conceal, this political concern by pointing to the difficulties of defining and identifying and then removing bad apples and to the possibility that acknowledging the flaws in some claimants, which might justify reducing their benefits, might also result in policies that deny them any benefits at all. These difficulties are discussed in chapter 5.

Such well-intended evasions, however, are in vain. Experience (and human nature) suggests that those who oppose programs to assist the poor will insist on raising the subject anyway, using it to discredit those programs (at least in their current form) and to redirect voters' limited altruism. The perverse result is that benefits will be denied to good and bad apples alike. The silence of redistributionists allows their opponents to frame the debate over bad apples. In contrast, a strategy of directly confronting the bad apples problem can produce significant policy improvements for good apples. For example, before PRWORA, opponents of welfare invoked "Cadillac welfare queens," deadbeat dads, and other bad apple stereotypes to force a fundamental reconsideration and reform of the policy. When President Clinton acknowledged that such individuals did participate in welfare programs, endorsed the condemnation of their behavior, and suggested that ultimately removing them from the welfare rolls was desirable, it became politically possible to mobilize the limited altruism of voters to produce a better policy, one designed to improve the prospects of most families previously dependent on welfare.[44] This reform in turn sharply reduced the public stigmatization of those who remained in the program, indeed even reduced the media's discussion of them, as our tabulation of welfare-related terms in the *New York Times* demonstrates.

Some resource misallocations are inevitable in programs directed at bad draws, but we think that the problems associated with bad apples and bad bets contribute to severe misallocations in some important contexts. For this reason, evasions of these problems are socially damaging and should be remedied in the interests of the vast majority of program beneficiaries. Moreover, speaking truthfully (as one sees it) is a cardinal virtue in a representative democracy.[45]

Sadly, the list of such evasions is long. One particular tragic example was the refusal of many leaders to heed the warnings in the highly controversial Moynihan Report about the disintegration of so many black families in the 1960s.[46] Other examples include the long-standing denial by many Italian groups that the Mafia has caused serious problems in American life, the refusal by much of the trade union movement to acknowledge that organized crime has infiltrated it in significant ways, and the Catholic Church's failure to confront the pathology of clergy sexual abuse.[47]

Even well-intentioned dissimulation about issues vital to governance carries severe costs, and any social solidarity that this dissimulation advances is to that extent artificial and fragile. Moreover, public cynicism often erupts when the truth comes out, as it almost always will in a contentious, competitive polity like ours.

Bad Policies

Like Tolstoy's unhappy families, bad policies are bad in many different ways. In this section, we first present what we hope is a useful, though certainly rough, taxonomy of bad policies. Some of these policy categories are bad primarily because they tend to compromise target efficiency; other policies are bad for other reasons. The section concludes by focusing on six pathologies that help cause poor targeting in a wide range of social programs.

Although the following list hardly exhausts the universe of bad policy categories, we suspect that any sophisticated policy analyst would include these fifteen types, while perhaps disputing some of the specific program examples cited in the notes.

The first eight categories (which overlap somewhat) affect a broad swath of areas, many of which have less to do with targeting than with other defects. They include policies that

—are so poorly enforced as to subvert their own goals,[48]

—entrench an inefficient or unjust status quo and retard innovation,[49]

—permit officials to continue programs that the private sector can do as well or better and at lower cost,[50]

—reduce or even bar competition in private goods,[51]

—create uncertainties that discourage beneficial investment and other welfare-enhancing transactions,[52]

—give officials too much discretion,[53]

—give officials too little discretion,[54] or

—threaten constitutional values.[55]

Seven more of these categories apply with particular force to the problem of poor targeting. These bad policies

—increase moral hazard for private actors or for governmental actors (discussed earlier in this chapter),[56]

—encourage self-destructive behavior by those who can least afford it (an extreme version of the previous category; see chapter 5),[57]

—are costly relative to the marginal effect that the policy seeks to promote (as with bad bets; see chapter 4),[58]

—indirectly harm the poor by wasting resources on bad bets (see chapter 4),

—directly harm the poor by failing to remove bad apples (see chapter 5),

—invite fraud and abuse (see chapter 5),[59] or

—redistribute wealth regressively (see chapter 2).[60]

All of these bad policy categories (and others that our readers may identify) reflect some deeper, recurrent pathologies in the policymaking process. Here, we discuss six of these pathologies that are most likely to subvert target efficiency: downstream redistribution, overspreading, in-kind benefits, superficial rights discourse, fear of blaming the victim, and ignoring invisible victims and opportunity costs.

Downstream redistribution. Policymakers generally attend only to a policy's ostensible first-order distribution of benefits and costs, ignoring how those costs and benefits—but especially the costs—are then spread to others. An increase in the minimum wage, for example, is first borne by employers, who will spread as much of that cost as possible to existing or potential low-skilled employees, either by reducing output or by substituting higher-skilled workers or machines for lower-skilled workers. Similarly, manufacturers redistribute the costs of product-liability rules to their shareholders, workers, and consumers.[61] Although spreading these liability costs to consumers sometimes improves social welfare, the distributive effects of this cost-spreading may be regressive or otherwise undesirable. This inattention to downstream redistribution often reflects a self-conscious political choice to disguise unpopular effects and conceal the ultimate cost-bearers. But often it also reflects the failure of policymakers to ask questions about a proposed policy's second- and third-order effects, which can be large, and the often formidable analytical difficulties in identifying, tracing, and measuring consequences beyond a policy's initial impacts.

Overspreading. Sometimes, policymakers distribute program resources so widely—and thus so thinly—that they cannot do much good for their recipients, particularly those in greatest need. This is a familiar cause of target inefficiency. Politicians often misuse egalitarian rhetoric in an effort to justify such resource-spreading policies. Pork barrel legislation and other programs whose political support depends on logrolling are common examples, but overspreading is by no means limited to those programs. For example, the Model Cities program enacted during President Lyndon Johnson's administration kept enlarging the number of communities receiving funds to the point that the funds available to the originally targeted communities were too limited to make a difference.[62] Much the same has occurred with Title I educational assistance. The homeland security program has engaged in a similar kind of self-defeating but politically safe overspreading.[63]

In-kind benefits. With a few important exceptions such as Social Security (Old-Age, Survivors, and Disability Insurance [OASDI]), Supplemental Security Income (SSI), the EITC, unemployment compensation, and TANF, social welfare programs distribute benefits in kind rather than in cash. (Some social programs distribute near-cash instruments, such as Medicaid cards, food stamps, and housing vouchers that restrict the benefit to certain kinds of eligible goods or services, while still leaving the recipients some choice of providers and products.) When programs distribute in-kind benefits, they mandate consumption patterns potentially different from those that the recipients might choose for themselves. Parents, for example, might prefer to purchase tutoring for their children with some of the resources that the program requires them to spend only on food, housing, or health care.

Several factors explain this legislative tendency to distribute benefits in kind. Voters want their tax dollars to be used to advance specific public purposes like health care, not to increase poor people's general purchasing power and discretion. Politicians fear that some recipients would use cash benefits for illicit products or in ways that otherwise subvert the legislative purpose. Industries lobby for programs to ensure that resources are used to purchase what these industries sell.

Although these factors may well justify certain restrictions on recipients' consumption choices, in-kind benefits have two important drawbacks. The utility loss to the recipients in using in-kind transfers may be quite large, and in-kind transfers may also offend our egalitarian goals.[64] Policymakers may reduce these disadvantages by allowing recipients to cash out their in-kind benefits under certain circumstances or to trade them, perhaps only in part, for other kinds of socially approved goods.

Superficial rights discourse. Many legal scholars and social scientists have called attention to the pervasiveness of discourse about rights in contemporary public debates. Usually, either they praise this "rights-talk" as a spur to broader legal protection of important individual or group interests, or they condemn it for fostering a militant, adversarial culture in which it is harder to reach common ground.[65]

Our concern here about rights-talk is different. We worry that it tends to deny, obscure, and distort the tradeoffs among competing values and goods. Plainly, those who engage in rights-talk often mean to exploit this tendency. Advocates of more health care, affordable housing, higher wages, and other desirable ends hope to strengthen their arguments by insisting on a right to these goods as a moral or even legal entitlement.[66] Such rights rhetoric is usually deployed by people who ardently wish to increase the availability of a particular type of good, often for defensible reasons. In this way, they may hope to finesse the hard issues that policymakers must inevitably face as they proceed from policy design to policy implementation—for example, how much of the good will be made available, at what level of quality, at what price in terms of other goods, and under which conditions of access. Indeed, a policy advocate's ability to obscure these tradeoffs in legislative, bureaucratic, or judicial policy debates is among the most valuable of political skills.

People may also have more self-interested motives for engaging in rights-talk, particularly when the advocate is also an economic provider of the good. It is no surprise, then, to find teachers claiming a right to better education for their students, farmers invoking a right to nutrition for the poor, doctors and unions of hospital workers demanding a right to health care, journalists defending a right to protect their sources, and academics extolling the tenure system. Needless to say, such a convergence of public and private interests in policy advocacy tells us little or nothing about the merits of either the rights claim or the policy.

Fear of blaming the victim. As we have already noted, those who wish to advance the interests of disadvantaged individuals naturally worry that admitting the existence of bad apples will make it easier for the opponents of social programs to discredit those programs by blaming the participants for their·own misfortune and by suggesting that most or all bad draws are in fact bad apples. A similar strategy of avoidance or denial may be used to protect bad bets from a slippery-slope argument. Once one has said that an individual who would receive very little benefit does not deserve resources, it becomes easier to say that another individual who would receive only a modest benefit also should not get the resources.[67]

Although a compassionate concern about false victim blaming is understandable and one that we share, we think that identifying bad apple victimizers as victims in place of the true victims (good apples) is a morally perverse inversion. It does not respect the poor, the vast majority of whom are good apples, much less advance their interests. Yet this inversion is so common that many people who support redistribution fear with good reason that if they denounce or exclude bad apples, they will be accused of victim blaming and other moral defects, when in reality they would be merely expressing an important, sometimes suppressed insight about the impediments posed by bad apples to the progress of other bad draws. A legitimate concern about victim blaming, particularly of bad apples, should not be used to avoid a candid appraisal of the injustices and inefficiencies that may result from allocating program resources to those whose misconduct prevents good apple participants from benefiting as much as they could.

Ignoring invisible victims and opportunity costs. Politicians' appeals and public policy are strongly biased in favor of protecting visible victims and subsidizing visible beneficiaries, often to the far greater disadvantage of invisible ones. Policy intellectuals often describe this conflict as one between identifiable victims and merely statistical ones.[68] The previous two chapters have presented some familiar examples. This bias seems to reflect a common psychological pattern: people tend to identify more with those who are vividly imperiled than with those who are members of an abstract, hypothetical, anonymous group, even though the latter may be equally or even more imperiled as a statistical matter. This powerful identification engenders greater moral urgency and reaffirms values that society cherishes. It also facilitates policymaking by anecdote.

A more ubiquitous version of the bias against invisible victims is the failure of policymakers to carefully consider the opportunity costs of their interventions—that is, the fact that by using the resources to assist the beneficiary group, they sacrifice the interests of other groups. In part, this failure reflects the heroic requirements of synoptic decisionmaking and the boundedness of our operational rationality.[69] But it also reflects the tunnel vision of policymakers, who tend to focus almost obsessively on the particular programs, politics, and constituencies for which they are responsible. Indeed, were they to contemplate transprogrammatic opportunity costs at all, they would probably conclude that such costs are someone else's responsibility. As the parodist Tom Lehrer has a German scientist say about his nuclear-tipped rockets, " 'Once they go up, who knows where they come down. That's not my department,' says Wernher von Braun."

This chapter has explored both the challenge and the promise of improved target efficiency. In the next three chapters, we attend to the practical implementation of our approach by closely analyzing the two recurrent targeting problems that are the main focus of this book: bad bets (chapter 4) and bad apples (chapter 5). Chapter 6 then explains how policymakers can best perform the predictions and make the sorting decisions required to avoid bad bets and to remove bad apples. Chapter 7 points forward to a way of better policies through better targeting.

4

Avoiding Bad Bets

B ad bets can be found in virtually every social program. Most of our analysis of the bad bets problem will concern choices made by health care providers. Health care (as Willie Sutton famously said of banks) is where the money is. But medical decisions also raise the most difficult ethical issues. Even so, it is important to note that the bad bets problem, *mutatis mutandis*, afflicts the provision of other social services. Thus, bad bets include the student who plans to attend college but is unlikely to learn much, the participant in a drug rehabilitation program who is highly likely to relapse, and the applicant to a job training program who is likely to drop out. They would be bad bets even if the condition causing their failure in the program were not their fault, as might well be true in the case of the struggling student. Indeed, any deep-seated inability of a bad bet to alter his behavior may make him even a worse bet than a bad apple who at least is capable of self-reformation.

Individuals, of course, do not neatly fall into the bad and good bets categories. As discussed in chapter 2, they are arrayed along a continuum with no clear dividing line that can tell program officials whether or not to give a costly medical procedure to an elderly individual in a certain condition. Obviously, an individual may be a bad bet for one program but not for another—as when society denies enrollment to a failing student in a junior college but would grant him a needed heart transplant. By the same token, one may be a good bet over a range of expenditures but become a bad bet beyond that range. For example, individuals under unusual stress may be good bets for two or three psychiatric visits but not for six or seven. Giving a paraplegic a motorized wheelchair may be a good bet, while providing a costly daytime attendant to further improve his life may not.

Although we define bad bets in efficiency terms, classifying someone as a bad bet and denying him program resources often also promotes a distributional goal—for example, society's desire to favor those who have received the worst draws. If these worst draws will derive the greatest benefit from a public expenditure, then people who are only mildly bad draws are likely to be relatively bad bets for that program. For example, if society wants public housing units to go only to families whose income (controlling for family size) is below some threshold, then classifying applicants as better or worse bets will enable the program to advance its redistributive goal of favoring the worst off.

In many cases, however, the worst draws are bad bets—for example, a potential heart valve recipient whose poor health makes him unlikely to benefit from the surgery; the comatose accident victim whose condition is unlikely to improve no matter how much money is devoted to her care; or the incompetent worker who is not likely to master the skills in a job-training program for the building trades. Here, society may use the classification even though doing so frustrates its distributional goal.

Few would propose that the government give college scholarships to students whose academic promise is very limited, yet these students are also the ones with the worst life prospects. If society looks not just at their present status but at their likely future income, people whose bad draws will likely keep them at or near the bottom of the income distribution for the rest of their lives should be excluded as bad bets. Most people accept this regressive distributional outcome because they believe that subsidizing failing students to attend college is very inefficient. This reasoning is like the battlefield triage that leaves some of the most seriously wounded soldiers to die.

Sometimes, however, society allows its distributional goals—some of which are ill-defined—to trump the bad bet determination. Because this can produce very costly, wasteful, and perverse results, it is essential for the public to understand the tradeoffs that are involved. The U.S. government, for example, generally awards kidney transplants first to those who have been on the waiting list the longest, even though statistically these recipients are most likely to be in the worst medical condition and thus are least likely to benefit from the organs. Such an allocation system has the virtue of keeping hope alive for those on the waiting list, but this could be better accomplished by allocating, say, 90 percent of the kidneys on the basis of benefits gained and the remaining 10 percent on the basis of who has waited the longest. Indeed, even a lottery that still gave bad bets a chance would be less wasteful than a system in which those waiting longer receive priority.

Excluding bad bets can sometimes be relatively easy to justify, as when benefits occur with a low probability. For example, many medical screening and prophylactic procedures offer benefits only to a very few people who cannot be identified in advance. Although doctors debate the age at which one should be screened for breast or colon cancer, a strong consensus favors denying mammograms to women at ordinary risk who are 35 and colonoscopies to 45-year-olds at ordinary risk. These individuals cannot expect enough benefit to justify their getting the test. Similarly, Americans are not routinely screened for hard-to-diagnose tropical diseases, even those that are dangerous if left untreated, because the cost would far exceed the benefits. In cases like these, the benefit-cost criterion easily carries the day, both analytically and politically.

Exclusion is somewhat harder, but still relatively easy, when virtually everyone is a bad bet. For example, the government has decided that no one (except those on experimental protocols) should receive an artificial heart until the technology improves. With current technology, staying alive on an artificial heart becomes a high expense–low quality existence. Indeed, when some policymakers anticipated this situation decades ago, they purposely slowed artificial heart development.[1] Such cases obviate the need for any discomfiting line dividing those receiving the treatment from those denied it; one cannot point to a neighbor who is a little younger or a little stronger and say, "He got the procedure, so I should too."

Alas, bad bets are usually harder to identify in advance. For most medical expenditure categories, individuals differ substantially as to the benefits that they would receive per dollar of cost. Unless everyone can receive sufficient benefits to justify the expenditure, some individuals will qualify as bad bets. In this chapter, we test the case for excluding bad bets by focusing on the common situation in which some people are good bets, some are bad bets, and those denied the resources resent the denial. The hardest cases for exclusion are those individuals with genuine need whose misfortune is beyond their control, but who are bad bets nonetheless. Many bad bets, of course, do bear some responsibility for their difficulties—for example, students who reject good advice to remain in school and drop out, thus becoming difficult to employ, or individuals who ignore health warnings and adopt poor personal health habits that lead to diabetes and high blood pressure.[2] Indeed, some bad bets for programs may also be bad apples; drug abusers, for example, who have lapsed after prior rehabilitation programs, are neither promising nor obviously deserving candidates for a new program.

At the opposite end of the spectrum, the category of bad bets can include those individuals so favorably situated relative to other potential participants that they will derive comparatively few additional benefits from the program. When bad bets lie at both ends of the spectrum, a kind of double adverse selection can impede a program's ability to produce good bets on average. For example, an agency that offers job training and placement services to low-income individuals must steer between two quite different selection dangers. Its Scylla is that those with the most severe employment deficits will tend to be among the most eager applicants, thereby increasing the cost of service per participant and reducing the number of those who can be trained and then placed in jobs. Its Charybdis is that those who could most easily get jobs on their own without the program may be the most aggressive in seeking its services, thus reducing its value added—like the A student who comes in for extra help just before the exam or the student who takes a course that teaches a foreign language in which he is already fluent.[3]

Morally and politically speaking, however, the bad bets who are the hardest to exclude are the many who are bad draws because they are simply unlucky. These good apples–bad bets are our primary focus here.

Even when society is convinced that individuals are bad bets, it can be hard to exclude them. Although bad bets, by definition, do not benefit as much as other bad draws from a social program expenditure, they still may derive some benefit. When officials choose between good bets and bad bets in allocating scarce resources, they must bear the anxieties of making what Guido Calabresi and Philip Bobbitt call "tragic choices"—a dilemma that is noted in chapter 3 and discussed again in chapter 6.[4] As we shall explain in chapter 6, drawing on the tragic choices concept, society exhibits profound ambivalence—indeed, it can amount to psychological denial—about assigning explicit priorities of this kind, because such a choice seems to undermine certain cherished social ideals. When the costs are modest, such finessing behavior might be worthwhile. In many instances, however, society can better affirm its ideals by avoiding choices that actually contradict and misrepresent these ideals, choices that waste resources that would yield more value helping other bad draws who are better bets.

The QALY Approach to Bad Bets in the Medical Arena

The medical arena provides our primary examples of bad bets. This context, in which many conditions are beyond an individual's control, presents the toughest challenge for our bad bets approach. Medical decisionmaking also offers a well-established, though far from widely accepted, methodology for comparing the benefits generated by different interventions. Those benefits are computed using a metric: quality-adjusted life years (QALYs).[5] Using this approach, a year of full function is scored as 1 QALY, and a year not alive counts as 0. An in-between state, such as a year in severe pain, might be scored as 0.5 QALY.[6] The QALY concept, although employed primarily in the health arena, can be extended to other areas such as education. A typical question that would be used in education would be: Does a person benefit if he experiences an unpleasant four years of education but improves his subsequent earning power by 15 percent?

Now consider a typical medical decision. Through no fault of her own, a patient suffers from pulmonary arterial hypertension (continuous high blood pressure in the pulmonary artery). She can be treated with two drugs: treprostinil or epoprostenol. The first drug is much more expensive but only slightly more effective than the second. Treating this patient with the first drug could improve her outcome, but only at a cost of $120 million a QALY. (See intervention "W" in table 4-1 below.) That same $120 million could yield vastly more QALYs if used in any number of other ways. The QALY analysis concludes that individuals with pulmonary arterial hypertension are bad bets for the more expensive drug.

Economists' efforts to estimate the value of a statistical life underscore this point.[7] Such estimates typically assess how much extra pay individuals demand to incur some risk, such as working at a dangerous job or living near a health threat. These estimates are based on market data rather than on interviews, and they attempt to consider identical individuals across situations of higher and lower risk. Most value-of-life analyses reach estimates in the range of $5 million to $7 million for a life saved.[8] This implies, conservatively, that spending more than $500,000 to gain a QALY amounts to a bad bet. The basis for this conclusion is that people who are saved in the types of interventions considered (for example, auto fatalities avoided) live for more than fourteen years after their lives are saved, which implies that the benefit is less than $500,000 a QALY gained ($7 million ÷ 14 years = $500,000 a year).

The savings from reducing or eliminating bad bets are illustrated in figure 4-1, which presents a hypothetical distribution of the cost to produce a

Figure 4-1. *Hypothetical Distribution of Dollar Cost per QALY*

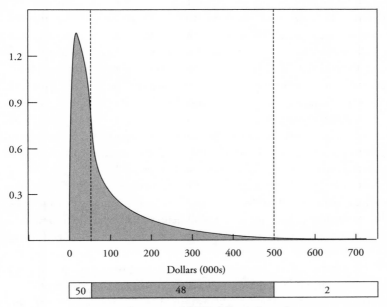

Density

Dollars (000s)

| 50 | 48 | 2 |

Percentage of QALYs falling in interval

QALY = quality-adjusted life year.

QALY for various combinations of patients and medical interventions. Note that the distribution is substantially right skewed, meaning that a very small number of cases (a case being a combination of a patient and a procedure) incur extremely high costs. This mirrors real life. Posit that the median expenditure for producing a QALY in a population is $50,000. Assume further that an expenditure of $100,000 to produce a QALY is as likely as one of $25,000, as would be true if the logarithm of expenditure were normally distributed.[9] The diagram shows a lognormal distribution where the 98th percentile entails an expenditure of $500,000 a QALY. Eliminating interventions that cost this amount or more to produce a QALY would eliminate the tiny area to the right of 500. This would save 16.2 percent of costs but only sacrifice 2 percent of QALYs. On average, the QALYs in that 2 percent would cost $748,000 each. This compares to an average cost of $79,000 a QALY for those below the $500,000 cutoff.

Consider how the dollars saved on those extremely high-priced QALYs could otherwise be spent. Even if we assume that most of the cost-justified medical expenditures have already been made, many other health-related efforts (for example, obesity prevention counseling) would yield many more QALYs per dollar. Table 4-1 illustrates this point.[10] The variability in the dollar-to-QALY ratio among possible medical interventions is dramatic. For any reasonable valuation of life, some of these interventions are clearly bad bets. All those interventions that produce QALYs at relatively low cost should be funded before society moves up the ladder to more expensive interventions.

For example, if society spent $4.2 million less on universal hepatitis C vaccinations (procedure B), one QALY would be lost. But if those same dollars were devoted to hepatitis screening (procedure C), 35 QALYs would be gained. For the same budget and by shifting resources for these two treatments, there would be a net gain of 34 QALYs. The vaccination approach is a poor bet relative to screening and thus is a bad bet overall.

Politically, this type of shift between different medical interventions is relatively easy to make. Because the high per-QALY cost of universal vaccination is due to the low probability that it will help, pressure for the program is likely to be limited, and individuals wanting the treatments will gain little support.

Tamoxifen treatment for women with high risk of breast cancer (procedures E, F, and G in table 4-1) presents a different story. The cost-to-QALY ratio for 60-year-olds and 35-year-olds is only 3 to 1. More important, the treatment is worthwhile for all three groups, given the $5 million value-of-life figure.

Such analyses must consider all categories of cost and of benefit. The calculations for interventions Y, Z, and AA, all of which involve transplantation of cadaver donor kidneys, ignore the fact that an irreplaceable resource, a kidney, is being "used up" in the transplantation. Thus the cost for Y (renal transplantation in a patient aged 65 or older) is really $73,000 a QALY plus one kidney. Suppose that this treatment yields 10 QALYs and that a successful transplant would produce 20 QALYs for a patient aged 40 to 50. Compared with the 65-year-old patient, the 40- to 50-year-old recipient would have additional lifetime medical costs, averaging $200,000. Thus giving the kidney to the younger recipient would gain 10 QALYs for $200,000, implying a cost of $20,000 per QALY gained, a very desirable outcome. This analysis suggests that health care officials should forgo intervention Y until all of the 40- to 50-year-olds have been treated. Similar analyses and calculations are possible for every entry in the table; its primary purpose is to show how QALYs figure in the analysis.

Critics of benefit-cost or cost-effectiveness analysis regard it as a tool for the stingy or hard-hearted, but that is false. In fact, it is a tool for disciplined

Table 4-1. *Cost per QALY for Various Interventions*

Intervention (Indexing letter indicates text reference)	Cost per QALY (2002 dollars)
Infectious disease	
A. Widespread pneumococcal vaccination versus no meningococcal vaccination in children presenting to the emergency room with meningeal signs.	$460,000
B. Vaccinating for hepatitis all chronic hepatitis patients aged 45 and older whose initial screens are negative for anti-HAV antibody.	$4,200,000
C. Universal screening for Hepatitis C virus in patients attending genito-urinary medicine clinics in United Kingdom.	$120,000
D. Testing whole blood donations with Nucleic Acid Testing for HIV, HBV, HCV, HBsAg, and the HIV p24 antigen in patients receiving one unit of whole blood from a single donor.	$7,900,000
Cancer	
E. Tamoxifen for primary prevention in women aged 35 at very high risk of breast cancer.	$45,000
F. Same as above, but for women aged 50.	$89,000
G. Same as above, but for women aged 60.	$140,000
H. Annual helical computed tomography screening for lung cancer in hypothetical cohort of current heavy smokers aged 60 who are eligible for lung resection.	$120,000
I. Same as above but in cohort of quitting heavy smokers.	$570,000
J. Same as above but in cohort of former heavy smokers.	$2,400,000
K. Bone marrow transplant from unrelated donor versus alpha interferon in newly diagnosed leukemia patients transplanted within one year of diagnosis.	$59,000
Neuropsychiatric and neurological conditions	
L. Use aggressive care but do not resuscitate or provide ventilation after third day of coma in low-risk patients who experienced nontraumatic coma.	$150,000
M. Treatment with interferon beta-1b versus treatment with mitox-antrone hydrochloride in patients with secondary progressive or progressive relapsing multiple sclerosis.	$690,000
N. Treatment with interferon beta-1b versus best practice without inter-feron in ambulatory patients with secondary progressive multiple sclerosis.	$1,900,000
O. Treatment with interferon beta-1b versus standard management in patients with relapsing/remitting multiple sclerosis.	$1,500,000
P. Breast conservation surgery for women aged 67 and older with radiation versus mastectomy in female Medicare recipients with stage I or II breast cancer and no previous cancer diagnosis.	$220,000
Cardiovascular	
Q. Admit to hospital for 24 hours then cardiac enzyme testing and exercise stress test if blood tests are negative versus observation of at least six hours, cardiac enzyme testing, and stress test if blood tests are negative in patients presenting to hospital with acute chest pain unexplained by trauma or chest radiological findings.	$180,000

continued on next page

Table 4-1. *Cost per QALY for Various Interventions (continued)*

Intervention *(Indexing letter indicates text reference)*	Cost per QALY *(2002 dollars)*
R. Deferring the decision for percutaneous coronary interventions to obtain a nuclear stress imaging study versus measuring myocardial fraction flow reserve to help guide decision for the intervention in patients with an intermediate coronary lesion and no prior functional study.	$840,000
S. On-pump coronary bypass surgery (with cardiopulmonary bypass) versus off-pump coronary bypass surgery (without cardiopulmonary bypass) in low-risk patients with predominantly single- or double-vessel coronary disease undergoing coronary bypass surgery.	$200,000
T. Coronary artery bypass graft and stent versus coronary artery bypass graft and angioplasty plus Abciximab for U.K. patients with coronary heart disease and angina who are expected to require revascularization.	$210,000
U. Duplex ultrasound screening without arteriography in 60-year-old patients with 5 percent prevalence of 60–99% asymptomatic carotid stenosis.	$1,700,000
V. CPR versus no CPR in patients with cardiac arrest.	$270,000
Respiratory	
W. Treatment with treprostinil for one year versus treatment with epoprostenol for one year in hypothetical cohort of 100 patients with pulmonary arterial hypertension.	$120,000,000
X. Lung transplantation versus standard care in patients with end-stage pulmonary disease who qualify for lung transplantation. (Excludes the shadow price of a lung that could go to other patients.)	$210,000
Genitourinary	
Y. Cadaveric donor renal transplantation with no wait versus continued dialysis in nondiabetic patients aged 65 and older who are stable on dialysis. (Excludes the shadow price of a kidney that could go to other patients.)	$16,000
Z. Cadaveric donor renal transplantation, same as above but with two-year wait. (Excludes the shadow price of a kidney that could go to other patients.)	$73,000
AA. Cadaveric donor renal transplantation, same as above but with four-year wait. (Excludes the shadow price of a kidney that could go to other patients.)	$210,000
Musculoskeletal symptoms	
AB. Rapid MRI versus lumbar X-ray in hypothetical cohort of primary care patients with low back pain referred for imaging to exclude cancer as the cause of their pain.	$300,000
Congenital anomalies	
AC. 3D CT scan versus conventional radiographs in children at low risk for craniosynostosis.	$7,600,000
Critical Care	
AD. Dialysis in seriously ill hospitalized patients with renal failure.	$160,000

Sources: See endnotes.

thinking and priority setting. Few readers, we suspect, would want to pursue the interventions in this table that cost more than $1 million a QALY. Such analysis should also be viewed as a weapon for those who are not in power, just as accounting empowers corporate shareholders. If officials are skimping on a program (for example, a program to prevent teenage pregnancy) that could save vastly more resources in the future, benefit-cost analysis may show that the program is worthwhile. Similar analysis will justify Tamoxifen treatment for breast cancer (E, F, and G) or bone marrow transplants for leukemia patients (K). Widespread screening or prevention programs are likely to be supported when careful attention is paid to their benefits and costs. Thus, the federal Advisory Committee on Immunization Practices recently recommended that

> all girls and women be given a new vaccine that prevents most cases of cervical cancer. . . . The vote all but commits the government to spend as much as $2 billion to buy the vaccine for the nation's poorest girls from 11 to 18. . . . [Studies showed that the vaccine] would save more in health expenses than the cost of buying the vaccine.[11]

In short, the vaccine saves both dollars and QALYs. Absent the type of analysis conducted for the cervical cancer vaccine, however, preventive programs will likely be underfunded because those who gain from them are hard to identify ex ante; these potential beneficiaries of the program are therefore less likely to demand the services. Annual eye or foot exams for diabetics, services that are inexpensive yet medically valuable, fit into this category.

Difficulties in Identifying Bad Bets

To illustrate the challenges facing a program official who is interested in avoiding bad bets, consider the example of Mickey Mantle and his liver transplant. (Leave aside the fact that he was also a bad apple because his liver problem almost certainly was caused by heavy drinking despite many warnings and much counseling and treatment.) Baylor University Medical Center, where he was treated, reported data to make his treatment seem reasonable. For example, Baylor claimed that it could give Mantle a 55 percent chance of surviving three years, that its preliminary tests were inconclusive, and that it learned only after the transplant that the cancer had spread, which seriously limited Mantle's life expectancy. The total costs, not counting a precious liver that could have been given to a better bet patient, were probably around $300,000.[12] After his death, some observers argued that Mantle's transplant was a good bet ex ante but that it simply had a bad outcome.

The example of organ transplants raises additional issues, such as how to secure the greatest net benefit for each organ used, since organs are scarce and cannot be reproduced simply by spending more money. The criterion might be total QALYs gained or total dollars expended. These two criteria might converge: people who would benefit the most from the transplanted organ are likely to be in better health and thus likely to require fewer resources for a successful transplant. Even considering lifetime medical costs based on a dollar-to-QALY ratio might lead to the same choice, because their initial costs for a transplant would be very high but would be spread over a longer lifetime.

To frame an appropriate policy in cases such as Mantle's, an analyst should have compiled a list of a few dozen people who appeared to be in a roughly comparable condition. If the majority really did survive for three years, if livers were readily available, and if postoperative costs were likely modest, then giving the liver to Mantle might have been reasonable.[13] These are strong ifs; it seems much more likely that better bets were available, that is, patients who would have received far greater expected benefits from the transplant.

Unfortunately, some people bristle at this sort of benefit-cost or cost-effectiveness calculation. Yet they would surely accept such an analysis in situations when the severity of the resource shortage cannot be denied. For example, battlefield medics use well-honed rules of thumb to make inescapable triage decisions about who can benefit most from the limited interventions that the desperate circumstances permit. Similarly, despite the Mickey Mantle case, people are more willing to accept prioritization for organ transplants, for which the supply is strictly limited, than to accept cut-offs on heart valve replacements. They may reason that pigs and plastic are in unlimited supply and that dollars are the primary constraint. But dollars too are limited, and as health care costs creep toward one-sixth of GNP, reducing the competitiveness of American firms and foreclosing other welfare-enhancing expenditures, the principle of "Give it to them if they benefit" is obviously not sustainable.

Nonetheless, few if any of our public or private health plans are explicit about prioritizing; for example, they do not impose any limits on costly procedures based on age or health status. Perhaps the policymakers and plan managers are relying on physicians to be vigilant stewards of scarce resources, a role that some advocates expected HMOs to play many years ago. If so, it is a vain hope. Physicians are notoriously poor gatekeepers. They possess powerful incentives (including ethical obligations; loyalty to their patients; a desire to gain a reputation for saving lives; knowledge that most of their patients will not bear many, or any, of the costs; and possible financial interests) that encourage them to allocate resources as if they were free and unlimited.[14] In fact, the medical profession is on record in favor of helping bad bets. According to the Code of Ethics of the American Medical Association (AMA), "Physicians have a responsibility to . . . safeguard the interests of patients in decisions made at a societal level regarding the allocation or rationing of health resources."[15] This ethic, if strictly followed by physicians and countenanced by society, would defeat the goal of cost-effectiveness in the delivery of medical care.

This attitude is reinforced by widespread insurance plans that cover all treatment costs, perhaps after a small patient copayment. This practice makes resources seem free for both physicians and patients. Yet, these resources are very costly to society. Cost-containment efforts, particularly in managed care organizations, seek to sensitize doctors to these costs, but as discussed in chapter 6, these efforts have largely failed, and political resistance to the rationing demanded by such efforts remains formidable. Resistance to health care rationing is, if anything, even stronger in Canada and the United Kingdom than in the United States.[16]

Even setting aside these social-psychological, political, and ethical obstacles to avoiding bad bets, deciding how to cope with the problem of bad bets in medical care is a challenging analytic task. First, the analyst needs detailed information about the patient's medical condition to determine that an individual with a certain condition who is being considered for coronary bypass surgery will cost on average $X and will yield only Y QALYs. Seeking such individualized information may raise privacy concerns, requiring the patient's informed consent or some other safeguard. (The privacy problem is briefly discussed in chapter 6.)

Second, the policy analyst needs a broad database capable of revealing the frequency and magnitude of the bad bets problem as shown by past outcomes. Unfortunately, detailed information about patients' outcomes is rarely available. Thus the analyst must use broad categories in reaching conclusions. Obviously, the inability to categorize the data more finely reduces the ability to identify outlier individuals, be they unusually good bets or unusually bad bets. For example, bone marrow transplants are rarely used on older cancer patients but might be quite worthwhile for an elderly individual who is otherwise in vibrant condition.

Third, if an analyst identifies particular cases or categories of bad bets, she merely reaps anecdotal evidence. She does not learn how widespread the phenomenon of bad bets might be. If their numbers are few, as discussed in chapter 2, society may wish to buy ethical comfort in a tragic choice, since that comfort is available at a manageable cost. Alas, for many medical situations concerning bad bets, large numbers of eligible recipients exist. Unless society can avoid the bad bets, vast resources may be spent unwisely.

Screening for Bad Bets

Given realistic data limitations, the best way to screen for bad bets is to identify broad categories of recipients who probably will receive only modest benefits relative to the resources they use. Sometimes potential beneficiaries—and thus potential bad bets—are not individually identifiable, because benefits flow to a relatively large and anonymous population, as with most environmental regulation.[17] But our focus here is on treatments that are *individually* delivered.

A recent study on the benefits of cholesterol-lowering therapies divided its population sample by age, sex, and four coronary risk factors. Using a previously validated computer-simulation model, the study compared the cost-effectiveness of diet interventions with that of treatment with statin drugs. The researchers concluded that "primary prevention with a statin compared with diet therapy [ranged in cost from] $54,000 per QALY to $1,400,000 per QALY."[18] Using a cost-effectiveness threshold of $100,000 per QALY, the study found that primary prevention with a statin was worthwhile for only 62 of 240 risk groups. Younger patients without risk factors, particularly women, gained the lowest benefits from such treatment. Given the high cost of medical resources, they are inevitably rationed, either implicitly or explicitly, and statins are not different. Indeed, many physicians already ration them, for example, by prescribing statins to older men over a broad range of conditions, but much less frequently to older women and only to younger patients with significant risk factors. Note that physicians ration statin therapy despite the fact that *all* of the groups reap some risk-reduction benefits from it.

The use of sex or age as a basis for rationing may be politically or even legally unacceptable in important contexts, even when that use has predictive benefits. For example, federal civil rights law prohibits the use of age as a screening tool in federally subsidized programs, subject to some broad exceptions.[19] The United Kingdom used to ration kidney transplants using an age cutoff. It no longer does so.[20] Indeed, the United Kingdom no longer uses age as an official consideration for any procedures. The notorious Oregon Medicaid prioritization system created a specific rank order in which health interventions were to be provided, with lower-ranked interventions essentially rationed out of use. Some interventions had ages attached; the same treatment might be provided to a 45-year-old but not to a 70-year-old. However, the administration of George H. W. Bush specifically prevented the

Oregon Medicaid program from using age as a factor in any context. Indeed, it had a more general objection to using QALYs because the QALY measure disfavored disabled patients. (There was no need to throw the analytic baby out with the protective bathwater. Disabled patients could be protected by requiring all QALY calculations to treat them as if they were able-bodied.) In the end, the Oregon system eliminated quality of life from its formal criteria for ranking treatments, and uses cost as a consideration only as a tiebreaker.[21]

The controversy over screening by age also extends to whether age is a good predictor of medical outcomes. Often those who disagree on this point are simply using different outcome measures—say, QALYs gained as opposed to short-term survival. Kidney transplants provide an important example. The Wake Forest Medical Center reports that the success of its transplants appears to be unaffected by age.[22] Even if this is so, a successful 85-year-old kidney recipient will gain many fewer years of life from the organ than will a 45-year-old, on average. Thus, he is a worse bet if QALYs is the proper measure, as we have argued. Consequently, an analysis of future life expectancy, or better still future QALYs, should be an important part of the effort to direct scarce resources to good bets.

Sometimes screening for bad bets will lead to the use of one drug rather than another. Celebrex is a celebrated anti-inflammatory drug, but over a broad range of conditions, the data do not support its greater efficacy when compared with traditional nonsteroidal anti-inflammatory drugs (NSAIDs), which are also much cheaper. Although Celebrex is easier on the gut, hence safer for patients with a history of ulcers, inconclusive evidence suggests that it poses a higher risk of heart attacks. In short, choosing Celebrex over an NSAID is often, but not always, a bad bet.[23]

Identifying Bad Bets and Assessing the Magnitude of the Problem

As table 4-1 and the accompanying discussion illustrate, two critical tasks are necessary to address the bad bets problem in the medical context: identifying the combinations of individual characteristics and treatments that constitute a bad bet and determining how frequently those combinations actually arise. The next two sections focus on medical expenditures in the last period of life and so-called futile medical care as exemplars of the kinds of analyses that take on both of these critical tasks.

THE LAST PERIOD OF LIFE. Critics often identify as wasteful medical expenditures made during the last period of life—say, during the last month or year. Their logic is that medical expenditures in this period can be shown to have accomplished little, and thus they must be bad bets. Unfortunately, however, we only know after the fact that a patient was indeed in the last month or year of life. Suppose, for example, that an expensive operation may restore full status but has a significant treatment mortality within a week. Retrospectively observing those who died quickly, one might mistakenly conclude that a large amount was spent for at most a week of life. The converse countervailing factor is that some people die suddenly without warning and thus at unexpectedly low cost. An example would be the vibrant 75-year-old who suddenly dies from a massive heart attack, thus using few medical resources during this final period of life. These two cases of surprise or sudden death—one using a lot of resources and the other a few—cut in opposite directions. If the second situation predominates, as we expect, this would imply that calculating expenditures in the last period of life underestimates the magnitude of the problem of bad bets.

In a series of articles, James Lubitz and others studied Medicare payments in relation to both longevity and spending during the last period of life. Longevity has increased rapidly in the United States, and this increase, along with the forthcoming population bulge from baby boomers, will challenge the fiscal soundness of the Medicare and the Social Security or OASDI (Old-Age, Survivors, and Disability Insurance) systems. Surprisingly, longevity per se does not add a great deal to Medicare spending. Thus, the estimated 7.9 percent increase in life expectancy beyond 65 years that will occur between 1990 and 2020 will only increase lifetime Medicare expenditures by 2 percent.[24] Estimated lifetime expenditures (in 1990 dollars) for people who die at the age of 80 are $56,000 but only $65,600 for individuals who die at 101 and older. Indeed, the payments associated with an additional year of life and annual payments both decreased as the age at death increased. This, of course, is good news. It is highly unlikely that we are just keeping large numbers of people alive in greatly reduced status, in which their health costs are high and quality of life low. In our terminology, people who live long lives are not bad bets, on average, even in their advanced years.

We turn now to spending during the last period of life.[25] All calculations were made using data from 1976 to 1988 and do not include drugs, nursing home expenditures, and expenditures for Medicare recipients under the age of 65, who are eligible because of disability. First, perhaps surprisingly, the older the individual was, the less was spent in the last year of life. In 1988, decedents (that is, those who died within that year) aged 65 to 69 averaged $15,436 in expenditures. By contrast, decedents aged 90 and older had expenditures of only $8,888. It may be cheaper to wear out than to die an untimely death. Alternatively, society may work out informal ways to spend much less money trying to save the quite elderly, conceivably because society or the individuals themselves or their doctors or families think that the investments are not worth making—even though the patients themselves are paying but a small share of the costs.

Leaving age aside, Medicare spends much more on its members in the last year of life than it does on typical members. Although decedents make up about 5 percent of the over-65 Medicare population, they made up 37 percent of the 5 percent of beneficiaries who incur the highest costs and 47 percent of the 1 percent of beneficiaries with the very highest costs. (As just discussed, this is not an age phenomenon; annual expenses generally decrease with age.) Overall, those in their last year of life use about 28 percent of the Medicare budget, roughly five to six times their proportional share. This percentage for the last period of life has not varied much in recent decades.[26] This would be appropriate if these individuals were receiving comparable benefits from these expenditures. But their lives are not being extended significantly (by definition), and it is unlikely that their quality of life on average is improved enough after the expenditures are made to justify this cost. These calculations are only suggestive; it is hard to know how many of these individuals in their last year of life might have had legitimate promise to be restored to reasonably good health, which would imply that ex ante they may not have been bad bets.

A more refined analysis is much more revealing. Examining expenditures at periods much shorter than a year before death yields a much more dramatic pattern, making the bad bets expenditures much more consequential. More than half of the spending for decedents comes in the last 60 days of life, and more than 40 percent comes in the last 30 days. This implies that one-eighth of the overall Medicare budget is spent on individuals in the last 30 days of life. These individuals are not only bad bets when considering resources used to produce a QALY, but they are sufficiently numerous to be a significant source of expenditure in absolute terms. (Such expenditures, both large and ineffective, are our prime policy concern.) Given the fact that death follows within a month, it seems quite unlikely that most expenditures on these individuals looked promising in terms of promoting either quantity of life or quality of life when they were undertaken. Significantly, all clinicians with whom we have discussed this problem confirm our sense that treating physicians are keenly aware of this poor prognosis but also state that their ethical, financial, psychological, professional, and other incentives almost all point toward providing interventions.

Curtailing expenditures that, viewed ex ante, are likely to be made in the last month of life strikes us as less problematic from an ethical perspective than many other possible ways of dealing with bad bets. First, it is even-handed; each of us will have a last month of life. Second, nonpalliative expenditures likely do little to promote either the quantity or the quality of life. (Many terminal patients choose hospice care, discussed below, to yield better quality of life and quality of death.) Third, physicians are likely to be in a better position to predict accurately the imminent demise of patients who in fact die within the month, when their lethal symptoms are probably more obvious, than they are for patients who in fact die within a longer period, say a year. Fourth, the resources can be used to help numerous other bad draws who are better bets. We suppose, therefore, that most people who understood these four propositions but who otherwise stood behind the Rawlsian veil of ignorance would probably favor a policy avoiding the unsystematic, wasteful allocations that are now being made in the last month of life.

FUTILE CARE. A second large group of bad bets are people who undergo futile care. The widely cited book by Schneiderman and Jecker defines futility as "any [medical] effort to provide a benefit to a patient that is highly likely to fail and whose rare exceptions cannot be systematically produced."[27] Futile care is often given to individuals in precarious and often uncomfortable conditions near the end of life.

One taxonomy divides futile care into three categories. *Physiologic futility* is using interventions that will not help—for example, prescribing antibiotics to treat a common cold.[28] *Qualitative futility* is more controversial, encompassing interventions that merely sustain unconsciousness or fail to end total dependence on intensive care.[29] An example is continuing artificial nutrition for a persistently comatose patient, as in the Terri Schiavo case.[30] Finally, *quantitative futility* is used for a situation when the probability of success for a given treatment is very low, usually less than 1 percent; an example is providing CPR to an elderly, terminally ill patient.[31]

The AMA identifies three common clinical paradigms of futile care: life-sustaining intervention for patients in a persistent vegetative state; resuscitation efforts for the terminally ill or for those with multiple organ failure; and aggressive therapy or surgery for advanced fatal illness without a realistic expectation of care—for example, hemodialysis, chemotherapy, or surgery for advanced fatal illness.[32] Apart from these paradigms, the medical literature contains multiple notions of futility, emphasizing both the quality-of-life aspects and the life-prolonging aspects of potential treatment.[33] Indeed, studies commonly provide conflicting definitions of futility within the same article.[34] But basically, the medical profession has defined futile care as interventions where the patient's expected benefit is zero or so minimal as to not justify any significant cost.

Determining when a treatment is medically futile is particularly difficult when some patients are expected to gain nothing from a treatment whereas others will likely benefit significantly and when there are no widely accepted criteria to determine who fits into which category. But taking seriously the principle of avoiding bad bets means accepting the need to find procedures and criteria for making such determinations. Chapter 6 takes on this task.

Health status indicators are a good place to start. But because the underlying prediction models, or the physicians' judgments attempting the same task, are probabilistic, many bad outcomes will look like erroneous predictions once the outcomes become known. Moreover, clinicians often disagree about whether a treatment is futile in a particular situation. One study of a small intensive care unit revealed at least one significant disagreement about the survival assessments for each of the majority of severely ill patients who ultimately died in the intensive care unit (ICU) or hospital ward. Similarly, in another study about life support decisions, the clinical staff disagreed in 48 percent of cases (family members and staff disagreed in 24 percent).[35] Indeed, even when clinicians agreed that a treatment would be futile, they disagreed about whether or not treatment should be withheld or withdrawn. Their decisions were even more divergent when predicting the future quality of life.

If medical futility is difficult to define, if it stirs disagreement in practice, and if it raises important ethical issues when used to guide treatment, one may reasonably ask whether it is worthwhile developing futility criteria. It is. First, futile care lies on the borderline between minimally beneficial and harmful treatment. Thus, failure to avoid futile care can actually harm some patients. Second, and more controversial, futile care wastes scarce resources. We know of no broad study of the overall cost of futile care, but there are estimates for some specific categories.

The hospice movement represents a significant effort to avoid futile and low-payoff care, while simultaneously aiming to improve the quality of life for a dying individual. An important recent study of Medicare decedents in two states concludes that hospice care can provide a significant cost savings for patients who eventually die from cancer—a reduction in medical expenditures of about 13 to 20 percent in the last year of life. Their analysis shows that at least for their sample (only a third of the cancer patients elected hospice care), patients with diseases other than cancer who went into hospice care actually had higher overall expenditures, which cancelled out the overall cost reduction achieved by hospice care.[36] A critical question, which this study did not answer, is whether and how much hospice care improved the quality of life and quality of death for these individuals.

Taken together, greater use of advance directives (discussed in the next section), hospice care for cancer patients, and less aggressive treatments would save an estimated 3.3 percent of total health care spending, which amounts to 6.1 percent of Medicare costs.[37] Hospice care and advance directives are estimated to save between 25 and 40 percent of health care costs during the last month of life alone.[38]

The goal of cost-effective health care may be gaining support. One study estimates that futile patients on Medicare—those who are predicted to die in the ICU—comprise only 13 percent of all patients but consume up to 32 percent of total resources.[39] Treating those patients is estimated to cost up to $210,423 each.[40] A hopeful sign is that a large and growing number of deaths in ICUs occur after a decision has been made to withdraw or withhold life support. A study of the University of California in San Francisco found that in 1988 about half of ICU deaths occurred this way, but by 1993 the figure had risen to over 90 percent.[41] A 1998 national survey found that the median institution limited life support in 70 percent of ICU deaths and that 48 percent of deaths followed withholding or active withdrawal of life support.[42] Doctors, it seems, are allowing more end-of-life bad bets to die in peace.

The extreme case of the medical bad bet goes beyond futile care to situations in which individuals can expect to actually suffer from treatment. Some of these negative-value treatments are widespread, and eliminating them could offer significant savings. The overuse of antibiotics in some clinical situations appears to be a case of a common negative-value treatment. A second example is cesarean sections that are performed in some localities at rates greatly exceeding those on comparable patients in other localities.

Strategies for Ameliorating the Bad Bets Problem

Here, five alternative approaches are considered for excluding bad bets from receiving medical services: encourage informed patient choice at the time of illness; foster physician awareness of the problem; implement broad-based policy changes that constrain physicians' natural tendencies to provide minimally beneficial, cost-ineffective services to their patients; expand research on which interventions are and are not cost-effective, specifying under which conditions and for which categories of patients cost-effective interventions should be used; and promote the use of informed patient precommitment through living wills.

Informed Patient Choice at the Time of Illness

Some patients may choose to forgo expensive treatment even if that treatment has some low probability of benefiting them under certain conditions. Recently, in the most extensive trial to date, Medicare gave just such a choice to emphysema patients. The treatment was surgery for lung volume reduction, whose use had been skyrocketing. The cost of the procedure, with recuperation, can be up to $50,000. Some projections estimated that the procedure could cost Medicare $15 billion annually. Medicare conducted a clinical trial that showed that the procedure has a 10 percent mortality rate and does not lengthen life for most patients.[43] When these facts were presented to doctors and patients, demand plummeted. In fact, from January 2004 through September 2005, only 458 patients received the treatment at a total cost of $10.5 million. Thus, "replacing anecdotal evidence with scientific data saved money and the lives of patients who were unlikely to benefit from the surgery."[44] Medicare is now pursuing the strategy of clinical trials and reporting on a range of treatments—for example, new cancer drugs, defibrillators, PET scans to detect early Alzheimer's disease, and home oxygen therapy for emphysema.[45]

Similarly, we suspect that many patients would decide to forgo late-stage treatments if matters were explained to them in a conversation such as the following:

> Despite our treatments, your cancer has continued to progress. Though we could try treatment with an alternate regimen, I think the likelihood of a significant response is low. Further, there is a significant risk of making you ill or even hastening your death from complications of this aggressive drug combination. I am concerned about the quality of life in your remaining time. As an alternative, we could stop your treatments at this time, providing hospice care when needed. You would continue under my care to the end, and your pain would be controlled.[46]

Currently only 1.6 percent of Medicare benefits go to hospice care, which suggests that a counseling approach might make a substantial difference in avoiding bad bets.[47]

Physician Awareness of the Bad Bets Problem

Those who make policy seldom implement it. The officials who formulate Medicare policy do not deliver services; physicians do. If Medicare were to address the bad bets problem by adopting criteria that determined who should receive which subsidized treatments, such criteria would necessarily be based on statistics for a population and would not address the specific situation for any particular individual. Ideally, policymakers will set general default rules, while the implementers (that is, physicians) will depart from these defaults only when their superior patient-specific information indicates that their patient is a good bet for the treatment. The danger is that the physician will engage in compassion-based or proximity-based moral hazard; thus, the patient might receive a treatment that is not worthwhile. This tendency would be reinforced by the physician's knowledge that the patient will bear little if any of the financial costs. This tension between using general categorical default rules and using beneficiary-specific information is by no means confined to health care programs; it is a central theme of chapter 6. There we propose an intermediate system, which employs an appeals process to produce better decisions than those emanating from a pure rule-based system or a pure individualized model.

With better information about cost-effectiveness and greater acceptance of the ethical justifications for prioritizing in response to it, physicians might be more inclined to initiate conversations about the likely futility of late-stage treatments and to refrain from ordering tests and treatments that are not cost-effective. A more radical option, probably not feasible or desirable in the present state of research, would be to expand the physician's duty to obtain informed consent to include making such cost-effectiveness disclosures in bad bet situations.[48] This would require the courts to support physicians in the event of malpractice claims or in situations when a family demands additional treatment that the physician denied because it was determined to be cost-ineffective.

Some gentle incentives might induce physicians to take greater account of the problem of bad bets. For example, in 2006 the Group Insurance Commission of Massachusetts, which insures state employees and is one of the largest employers in New England, extended its Clinical Performance Improvement Initiative to physicians. It required the seven health plans it offers to divide doctors into two tiers on the basis of both quality and efficiency, with the latter defined as cost-effectiveness. Patients will have lower per-visit copayments if they go to Tier 1 physicians. The copayment differences and the public identification of which doctors are in Tier 1 and Tier 2 are expected to spur doctors to more cost-effective behavior.

In another case, physicians in Green Bay, Wisconsin, cut the city's rate of cesarean sections by 30 percent over an eight-year period, prompting the following observation: if the current national rate moved down "half-way toward Green Bay's rate, there would be 250,000 fewer C-sections each year in the U.S., with decreased pain and surgical complications for mothers, shorter lengths of stay in hospitals, decreased repeat C-sections in later pregnancies, and probable financial savings of over $3,000 per delivery, or a total of $750 million nationally per year."[49] Cesarean section rates vary dramatically across geographic areas with no better natal outcomes where they are prevalent, which indicates overuse. The C-section evidence suggests that a number of procedures for a great variety of conditions may be given to individuals who would be better off without them.

Numerous studies document that treatments are used with highly varying frequencies in different locales in the United States and that when particular medical specialties prevail in a particular community, the specialists provide more and more intensive treatments than in other communities.[50] The same pattern has been observed in hospitalization rates, lengths of stay, and other dimensions of health care.[51] This suggests that specialists sometimes disserve their patients, delivering procedures that are not worthwhile to the patient but that are profitable to the physician.[52] Together, physican education and incentives could help counteract these temptations.

Broad-Based Policy Changes

Certain policies could effectively limit bad bets in health care. New reimbursement arrangements, for example, could dramatically change medical practice. The introduction of Medicare's Prospective Payment System (PPS)—paying providers on the basis of patients' conditions, not on the treatments they receive—led to significant changes in how hospitals were used during the last 90 days of life. Researchers found a sharp PPS-related decrease in the number of in-hospital deaths and a substantial rise in home-care, office visits, and the use of out-patient equipment.[53] The researchers present no evidence of whether the dying patients and their families benefited from or preferred the new pattern, but it evidently did not stir great protest or ethical controversy. This example suggests that indirect cost-control measures that reduce expenditures on bad bets need not engender a political backlash.

Another way to reduce costs is to refuse reimbursement for tests that have little expected value but can lead to expensive treatments. A prostate-specific antigen (PSA) test for an asymptomatic man in his late 80s may exemplify this. Even if he gets a high score, indicating the presence of cancer, his best course is probably just watchful waiting. But if he is tested and gets a positive result, his doctor will likely require more tests, a biopsy, and perhaps even treatment that the patient would have forgone before his test had he anticipated the outcome. Such a treatment is unlikely to improve his quality or quantity of life. If an ex ante assessment of a test suggests that it will likely lead to treatments for which the benefits are few (or negative) and costs high, then a policy generally barring the test would be sound. The fact that 1 patient in 100 would gain a substantial net benefit from the test does not affect this conclusion—unless such an individual can be identified with reasonable probability ex ante, in which case he should of course be given the test.

This analysis focuses on identifying combinations of patient conditions and treatments that represent bad bets, and seeking ways to avoid them. Thus, apart from its discussion of hospice care, it finesses the question of who should produce what care. In fact, production technologies, costs, and outcomes differ substantially across producers, both within types (for example, hospitals) and across types (for example, home versus hospital dialysis). Treating a patient in an inappropriate locale is a bad bet, since the dollars entailed could accomplish more elsewhere. Michael Porter and Elizabeth Teisberg, business school professors who are experts on competition, strategy and innovation, outline the enormous potential for creating results-oriented "value-based competition." They cite numerous instances where changed producers or production technologies improved both the quality and efficiency of care.[54] This raises the more general future research question as to what general reimbursement arrangements might alleviate the bad bets problem.

Research on Cost-Effectiveness

Policymakers should subject most common medical interventions to much more extensive cost-effectiveness analysis. This would promote evidence-based medicine, a goal that is frequently expressed but too rarely implemented.[55] It would enable all who affect the treatment decision to know which procedures are likely to provide significant benefit and which are not. As this evidence accumulates over time, we would expect many innovative responses. Insurance plans, whether publicly supported or private, for example, might state in advance that they will not pay for specified high-cost procedures of low or uncertain value, just as they often do for procedures regarded as still experimental.[56] This would benefit all the members of the general public who ultimately pay the bill with their taxes, their premiums, or their reductions in wages. This assumes, as almost all health economists agree, that the costs of employer-provided insurance come out of wages. Employers, unions, and consumers could take these insurer decisions on treatment coverage into account in choosing among competing health plans.

Patient Precommitment

The first strategy we discussed would ask doctors and patients to decide, when the patient is already seriously ill, whether to proceed with a treatment even though it is unlikely to provide much or any benefit. By that time, however, it is often too late. Living wills allow people to make choices earlier, at a time when they are likely to be in a better position to make rational decisions and to commit to those decisions. Living wills state the conditions under which individuals will decline future medical treatment; this precommitment is usually very broad because of the difficulty of predicting which specific illnesses will arise. Although a competent patient is always free to reverse the provisions in the living will, the fact that she has already thought about them and knows that they were made with a clear mind free of the pressures and stresses of serious illness makes her more likely to stick with them.

We suspect that significant savings could be garnered if living wills were more widely used—even as we recognize that people who actually face the life-or-death decision may think better of their earlier decision and revoke it. Although living wills may not help much with treatments that generate positive QALYs on average but that are still not cost-effective, they can help to curtail interventions that yield negative QALYs. Perhaps most important, they force people to think hard about these tradeoffs at a time when they can be most rational about them. Although many health plans now attempt to publicize living wills and many hospitals require patients to consider them upon admission, such efforts fall far short. A hospital requirement that a patient consider a living will accomplishes nothing for the individual who arrives with brain damage from an auto crash. Medicare and Medicaid could present a broad selection of optional living wills as part of their initial enrollment processes, and private health plans could do so on a regular basis. Employers, unions, and public health groups could hold focus sessions on the subject. Such precommitments could avoid some deplorable outcomes in which the patient suffers needlessly and significant costs are incurred.

Each of these five strategies can be carried out clumsily or deftly. Although all of them can be implemented in ways that raise ethical concerns, it is important to emphasize that the ethical values cut both ways. Denying people treatments that they want is troubling. However, when careful data-based analysis gives society strong reason to believe that individuals are bad bets for particular treatments, it also seems morally wrong for society to spend scarce resources to provide such treatments. To do so would deny the resources to better bets with equally or more compelling claims to society's solicitude as bad draws. The ethical arguments, then, are complex, and we do not say that we have resolved them. We claim only that default rules and guidelines might ameliorate them. Anticipating problems can sometimes enable society to reduce or avoid them, as the artificial heart example discussed earlier demonstrates. If there are fewer but sufficient CAT scan machines in a community, society can be confident that they will be used more sparingly and, one hopes, more wisely.

Nor must denial of benefits be an all-or-nothing situation. With transplants, for example, individuals who are in worse physical condition and are relatively bad bets might be given inferior organs—for example, from deceased donors who were older or who suffered more ailments at the time of death.[57] Most health plans routinely deny individuals access to experimental protocols, even those with dread diseases, unless the individuals are part of a scientifically valid experiment. Denials such as "We don't do that procedure here" or "the treatment is experimental and unproven" are probably more acceptable than "We won't give that treatment to you because it is expensive, and you wouldn't benefit much from it."

Hard Choices and Tricky Politics

Denying services to bad bets will never be easy. Most bad bets are good apples and often the kind of good apples with whom voters can easily identify and sympathize. These bad bets could even be their own relatives or themselves at some point. In this section, as with the earlier discussion in this chapter, we use medical care as our most important example of these hard choices, while emphasizing again that such choices are by no means confined to this policy domain but plague any social program that serves populations whose members have diverse prospects for success.

With medical care, many bad bets are bad bets simply because they are old or sick and thus have fewer QALYs left. Evidently, some physicians use age as the primary factor to deny individuals heart valve replacements (to go back to our common example).[58] Almost all voters can anticipate experiencing old age themselves, and they can also anticipate that steady advances in medical technology will continue to provide costly but beneficial drugs, treatments, devices, and other interventions that they will want for themselves. At some point, however, taxpayers may find the burden of funding these interventions more than they can, or wish to, bear. Rapidly aging societies like Japan and most of Western Europe may soon reach this point, although the tradition of making bad bets is deeply entrenched in these societies—not just in public attitudes and among policy elites but also in the courts.[59] Even in the United States, whose younger population reduces the bad bets problem, this point is bound to be reached, albeit decades later.

From an ethical point of view, taxpayers' almost universal anticipation of old age supports the legitimacy of using age in the eligibility decision. From a pure standpoint of quality-adjusted life years, medical condition is a better predictor of benefits than is age, but age as a criterion has major advantages: it is readily measurable and objectively evenhanded. So we shall use it for illustration. Unlike policies that disadvantage racial groups, people with different sexual orientations, or other minorities whose characteristics or preferences are clearly distinct from those of the majority, a policy that disadvantages the elderly is far less likely to be mean-spirited or animated by hostility, to represent a we-versus-they barrier, or to be otherwise invidious.[60] After all, the elderly are not only our parents and grandparents; they are also us, as we will (all too soon) become. To disadvantage the elderly, then, is in a real sense to disadvantage ourselves at a future point in time that we all earnestly hope to reach.

Of course, a fear of aging is widespread in American society, and intergenerational relationships can be fraught with tensions. Making decisions that implicate our identities across multiple time periods in the future—here, younger voters projecting their own frailty and vulnerability many years hence—is psychologically complex and epistemically problematic.[61] Still, the optimal condition for making hard collective resource allocation choices that provide disproportionate resources to various groups arises precisely when voters know or suspect that they may themselves experience the full consequences, good and bad, of those choices. This foreknowledge can create an uncommon self-discipline, highly salutary in a democracy like ours, that can encourage voters to make relatively wise, disinterested, egalitarian, and public-spirited decisions.[62]

The elderly constitute a large, growing, and highly effective voting bloc fully capable of protecting its group interests. This provides additional assurance that policies that steer away from elderly bad bets are unlikely to be adopted for hasty, ill-considered, or invidious reasons. If anything, the greater danger may be just the opposite: the elderly are so politically powerful that no policy that they think will adversely affect them is politically viable, regardless of how socially beneficial and fair the policy might seem to others.[63] Indeed, one can make a strong case that social programs disproportionately favor the elderly to the disadvantage of children. Political scientist Jacob Hacker observes, for example, that "U.S. social programs are more skewed toward the aged than in almost any other nation. The United States doles out nearly 40 times as much per senior citizen as per child and working-age adult."[64] The political struggles over the reforms of Social Security and Medicare reveal the formidable extent of senior power.

Many bad bets, of course, fall into groups that lack the political influence of seniors. Although politicians find it easier to limit the flow of resources to the nonelderly poor and to other marginalized groups, explicit rationing even for these groups is almost always a hard sell. Nevertheless, some rationing is usually unavoidable, and programs engage in it more or less openly. For example, health plans may limit the use of expensive drugs to priority conditions rather than extend them to all conditions that could conceivably derive some benefit.[65] Fiscally pressed schools make hard choices among the growing number of students who are thought to have special needs for individualized tutoring and other services that require additional resources.[66] Even groups that receive benefits primarily on the basis of a past disadvantage must often engage in this kind of prioritization. For example, Indian tribes that are allowed to conduct gambling operations require that individuals who wish to share in the proceeds prove a certain fraction of tribal blood. Thus individuals with one-eighth tribal blood may be included, but those with one-sixteenth excluded.

Our analysis suggests, then, that well-targeted redistributionists should want to avoid bad bets so as to redirect the vast social resources that bad bets now consume to the presumably far more numerous bad draws who are good bets. In some contexts, bad bets may be more numerous than good bets, for example, in programs with chronically high recidivism rates, such as many drug rehabilitation clinics. Eliminating bad bets in such programs would free far more resources for the remaining beneficiaries.

In nonmedical social programs, officials deny service to bad bets—applicants to state colleges, job training programs, and drug rehabilitation clinics, for example—without much social hand-wringing, and they often use age as a screening variable. Most professional schools will accept a 25-year-old applicant ahead of a 45-year-old, even if the schools expect the latter to perform better in the program and even at some risk that the denied applicant will file an age discrimination claim.[67] Even job retraining efforts for laid-off workers are more profitably directed at 30-year-olds, who have three or four decades of working life left, than at 60-year-olds. It strikes us as odd, then, that bad bets for increasingly scarce health care resources should be treated differently, much less that some policymakers would consider this approach unethical.

Even where the rationing procedure is less vivid or troubling than it is in medical triage, officials are likely to shrink from the task. Thus, they fudge their hard choices, make them seem less tragic than they really are, and sometimes just dole out money to avoid the discomfort. The federal government allocates substantial financial aid to college students with little effort to weed out those who are unlikely to succeed at school or to repay their loans. The many bad bets among these borrowers, as evidenced by high default rates, in effect deny needed funds to the many more who could use them better and would be more likely to repay. (In fact, recent tougher practices, what the Department of Education refers to as "enhanced management and oversight," have cut default rates substantially.)[68] Society deludes itself in thinking that all high school graduates should go on to college, when in truth good vocational training would serve many of them far better. In situations in which student loan programs do cover vocational training, the government's costs are far lower, even taking into account the very high default rates.

In exploring the limits to society's tolerance for bad bets, the scale of a bad bet (and thus how likely society is to view the choice as tragic) can matter. We introduced the example of conjoined twins in chapter 2. Because this condition occurs only once in 100 million births, bearing the enormous cost of separating them (often regardless of their nationality) offers society a relatively cheap way to reaffirm the values that it thinks it wants to reify, although it might make a different choice if such births instead occurred once in 100,000 births—a distinction that ethicists concerned with this case seem to have ignored.[69] Similarly, if miners were trapped much more often than they actually are, society might also choose differently. When rescues are rare, then, society is more willing to pay the relatively low cost to avoid the social obloquy of seeming heartless. But that cost, tolerable as a relatively unique case, at some point becomes unacceptably large when repeated. Social policymakers should think harder about what that point is and how to tell when society has reached it. And they should think harder still when the bad bets they are making also involve bad apples like Mickey Mantle.

Although policymakers are reluctant to make hard choices to avoid bad bets, they are more willing to do so when the shortage in a particular resource is so severe and obvious that everyone accepts the need for rationing, tragic though that decision may be. In less compelling situations, other factors seem to affect whether and how stringently society excludes bad bets. The most important of these factors is predictive accuracy.

The predictive accuracy of bets along with their sensitivity and legitimacy are prime topics in chapter 6. Here we briefly foreshadow that discussion. The instruments used to screen for bad bets and the factors used as predictors must be broadly acceptable. Sometimes, the observable characteristics that can help program officials determine who should receive resources are correlated with socially sensitive variables, such as race or gender, which are deemed too controversial to use as a basis for classifying an individual as a good bet or bad bet. Society might decline to use race as an eligibility criterion even if it were a strong predictor of success in a very costly program and even if substitute criteria, such as whether the individual had failed in prior programs, still left race as a good predictor. Race might not be used for a number of legal, political, and moral reasons. We might worry about the legitimacy of a race-based classification if it might be unconstitutional or if using race as a proxy might reflect or even reinforce the same discriminatory environment that made it a good proxy for predicting bad bets in the first place.

The use of race, however, might be more acceptable if used as a screening device for diagnosing certain medical conditions, for which race is a good, though not a perfect, genetic marker. Recent objections on ideological grounds to a hypertension drug directed to and distinctively effective for African Americans are misguided and can only serve to discourage research for treatments for this already under-served group.[70] We discuss race issues more generally in chapter 7.

Some characteristics are not inherently or generally sensitive but may nevertheless be considered to be illegitimate indicia of a person being a bad bet in certain circumstances. For example, in chapter 5, which focuses on bad apples, the reader will see that public housing agencies sometimes exclude families if a family member has engaged in certain kinds of criminal activity (that is, this family is a bad bet for neighborliness). Although the Supreme Court has upheld an extension of this policy, many who believe that it is unfair to visit the sins of the son upon his family continue to challenge the policy's legitimacy.[71]

Our discussion of the bad bets problem reveals that it makes choices hard for three reasons:

—Most bad bets are good apples, who are usually being denied positive benefits not because of something they did wrong, but just because the benefits to them are not large enough relative to their costs.

—Even when bad bets are obvious, politics often intrudes to impede or override rational decisions.

—In situations concerning bad bets, policymakers—like the rest of society at times—often live in denial.

The basic lesson of this chapter is that society should face reality. Policymakers should be willing to exclude some individuals from social programs, even when the excluded are in unfortunate circumstances through no fault of their own. Society must recognize that such exclusions are socially desirable given the reality of scarce resources, particularly in the medical context, where resources are becoming scarcer relative to growing social demands. As discussed, a lack of realism—or candor on the part of those who understand these lessons but are afraid to acknowledge them publicly—leads social programs to make too many wagers on bad bets. These bad bets—to expand a La Rochefoucauld maxim on hypocrisy—are the tribute that society's poor choices sometimes pay to its abstract moral ideals but more often pay to lazy thinking and political cowardice. Target efficiency and better bets are the unacknowledged victims of these poor choices.

5

Removing Bad Apples

Social programs often include a significant number of bad apples, individuals who impose large costs on good apples both in and out of the program, as well as on taxpayers generally. We maintain that these programs should seek to identify bad apples and then to remove them from the midst of the good apples. By improving the fairness and target efficiency of programs intended to benefit the good apple participants, removal would lead to more generous support for such programs among the numerous voters who are well-targeted redistributionists.

Few policy intellectuals are willing to examine the bad apples problem closely. Yet most people who are as poor as or poorer than bad apples strongly condemn their misconduct. Indeed, public opinion polls find that low-income and black respondents are more disapproving of deviance, disruption, and violence than are higher-income and white respondents (although the former are more cynical about the police).[1] Even more important, good apples manage to avoid engaging in such misconduct. Their good behavior often entails self-sacrifice—for example, the discipline to resist temptation and the courage to stand up to bullies. This fact, which is widely overlooked by advocates for the poor, needs emphasis. Every social policy should be designed to support the hard-won achievements of good apples, and every well-targeted redistributionist should seek to reward those achievements, not undermine them.

Unfortunately, rewards often flow to the wrong people, the bad apples. For example, Malcolm Gladwell describes social programs designed to help bad apples among the homeless move into their own apartments and rebuild their lives under the supervision of a special team of social workers. The moral and fiscal defects created by this approach are exemplified by a man named Murray—a chronic substance abuser who requires repeated emergency room care, social work interventions, and benign police monitoring and handling. "Thousands of people in the Denver area," Gladwell points out, "no doubt live day to day, work two or three jobs, and are eminently deserving of a helping hand—and no one offers them the key to a new apartment. Yet that's just what the guy screaming obscenities and swigging Dr. Tich gets. When the welfare mom's time on public assistance runs out, we cut her off. Yet when the homeless man trashes his apartment we give him another."[2] Gladwell goes on to assert that this approach has no moral justification but is "just about efficiency."[3] He is right about its moral incoherence—it sends precisely the wrong signal, both to Murray and to others facing hard choices about how to behave—but he may be wrong that it is efficient. As noted in our discussion of moral hazard in chapter 3, whether it is efficient or not depends on the magnitude of the additional costs incurred by encouraging the unwanted behavior.

A number of programs, we believe, have gone too far in seeking to be fair and responsive to their bad apple recipients. To develop sound policy for dealing with bad apples, we must understand who they are. Thus we begin by discussing the general criteria that should be used in defining bad apples and the difficulties surrounding any definition. We then present three specific sites of bad apple conduct—public schools, public housing, and homeless shelters—and analyze the different kinds of harms that these bad apples impose and the various remedial strategies available for reducing these harms.

Who Is a Bad Apple?

In chapter 1, a bad apple is defined as an individual whose irresponsible, immoral, or illegal behavior in the past—and likely in the future as well—causes good apples in a particular program to benefit less than they otherwise would. This preliminary definition serves our analytic purposes but must be rendered somewhat more precise if it is to be administratively and legally useful in any specific program. Our purpose here is to analyze some of the pivotal issues that must be addressed in any effort to develop program-specific solutions to the bad apples problem.

As noted in chapter 3, bad apple conduct is not a simple binary variable; it falls on a continuum. The bad apple characterization is defined by behavior and its effects on good apples, and both (the behavior and its effects) are continuous variables. For example, even when defining crimes—a much narrower category than that of bad apples—policymakers routinely distinguish between the violent and the nonviolent, the first-time offender and the recidivist, the hit man and the mere lookout man. Indeed, the law even differentiates among criminals who kill—for example between murder 1, murder 2, manslaughter, and so forth.[4]

The harm that bad apples inflict on others, and often on themselves, occurs only probabilistically, not absolutely. This is true not only in the sense that a person's life opportunities and behaviors are shaped in part by the fortuity, say, of who his or her parents were, but also because luck can determine whether a given bad or risky behavior actually yields a bad outcome.[5] A college student who engages in recreational binge drinking is unlikely to become an alcoholic in later life, but his irresponsible conduct, which may only be episodic, certainly increases the risk of bad outcomes during college. Whether he injures someone when he drives home inebriated or instead reaches his destination without incident depends on a number of contingencies, such as whether someone is coming the other way when he happens to weave. Similarly, whether a teenage girl becomes pregnant in a given sexual encounter may depend on the male's sperm count or the effectiveness of the contraception, which are in effect matters of chance.

From one perspective, it seems questionable to say that the student and the teenage mother are good or bad apples when their outcomes depended on factors that were beyond their control. From another perspective, however, their earlier choices to engage in certain activities increased the risk of bad outcomes. The probabilistic nature of outcomes for bad apples implies that the distinctions that policymakers must make, including any moral distinctions that turn on predictions about bad outcomes, will often be matters of degree, not kind, and will be to some extent arbitrary. This makes their determinations about bad apple status even more challenging and more controversial.

Bad apples' misconduct may be caused by factors other than their own bad choices. We never know with certainty why individuals are bad apples. Might the recidivist alcoholic who repeatedly consumes scarce mental health resources have inherited a strong familial propensity to drink? Is a school bully no longer a bad apple because he was abused by his parents or ingested lead paint as a young child? The possibility that someone who cannot readily change his behavior might be classified as a bad apple is morally troubling. These scruples are only magnified by research suggesting that certain conduct that society condemns as self-destructive—substance abuse and overeating, for example—is to some extent genetically determined. The fact that society cannot yet determine that extent, and indeed may never be able to do so, particularly for any given individual, further complicates the matter.

These moral dilemmas about causation and free will, of course, go back to the ancients. Even so, society has devised reasonable ways to manage these difficulties. It deploys two useful criteria for making such judgments: irremediability and intentionality. An individual who continues to misbehave even after having been warned or punished is more likely to be a bad apple, and a chronic one at that. Thus warnings and second (and sometimes third) chances are essential mechanisms through which society signals both its condemnation of the misbehavior and its definition of a bad apple, while simultaneously urging self-reformation. In the same way, the nature of misconduct often signals whether or not it is remediable. Intentionality, of course, is a familiar moral, legal, and cognitive category that bespeaks choice, agency, and probability.

But even when irremediability and intentionality are present, classifying someone as a bad apple is not morally straightforward. The chronically disruptive student may be suffering from attention-deficit disorder, seeking the attention of peers or adults, reflecting a genetic condition, or acting out a trauma caused by his dysfunctional family—conditions that may or may not be remediable in the short run or perhaps ever. Another kind of moral ambiguity arises when these two criteria cut in different directions. Conventional morality, we suspect, tends to consider the attention-seeking disruptive student more reprehensible—but also more remediable—than the genetically predisposed one. Recognizing such uncertainties, chapter 6 discusses how social programs can most accurately and fairly predict and classify bad apples (and bad bets), in part through well-designed appeals processes. But we must reiterate here a point made in chapter 2: policymakers should accord the highest social priority to improving outcomes for the good apples, even as they attempt to address the causes of bad apples' problems.

Harms Caused by Bad Apples

Bad apples in social programs inflict different kinds of harms. Although often conjoined, these problems are distinct analytically and perhaps operationally. Three sometimes overlapping categories of harm are discussed here: direct harm to good apples in the same programs, reduction of political support for programs designed to assist good apples, and fraud and abuse. For reasons explained below, we devote little attention in this book to fraud and abuse despite the enormous resources that those misbehaviors consume.

Direct Harm to Good Apples

Surely the most socially pernicious effect of bad apples is to injure the good apples in a program. In addition to the public schools and public housing programs discussed below, important examples of such injury include prisoners who assault peaceful prisoners or guards, HIV+ individuals who willfully fail to use the condoms or clean needles given to them by public health officials, and recidivist substance abusers who plague their families and communities and whose frequent readmissions drain scarce public hospital resources, including much-needed public hospital beds and rehabilitation program slots.

Sometimes, the harm is inflicted because of a perverse incentive contained in the law itself. Before 1996, for example, nondisabled children who misbehaved in certain ways could qualify for SSI benefits. With possible parental encouragement, many misbehaved. Congress then amended the law to provide that the individualized functional assessments prepared for children in the SSI program should prevent parents from gaming the system in this way.[6]

Reducing Political Support for Social Programs

By inflicting direct harm on good apples, stigmatizing them, and engaging in self-destructive conduct, bad apples tend to reduce political support for the programs in which they participate. In chapter 2, we characterized this harm as a negative reputational externality, noting that it places strains on the limited altruism of even those voters who favor some redistribution to the poor, and in chapter 3, we showed how better targeting to remove bad apples can reduce this stigma and increase support for the programs. Bad apples can also reduce political support when their misconduct spills over into more public spaces—for example, in parks, subways, or libraries—where other citizens perceive them as a public nuisance.

Fraud and Abuse

As we note in this chapter, service providers may be bad apples—often on a massive scale, as in the Medicaid and Medicare programs where they may bill for services not delivered.[7] The same behavior tips over to the demand side: some bad apples claim benefits for which they are clearly ineligible. For example, an audit found that 62 percent of those reimbursed under a post-9/11 program to subsidize air conditioners, filters, and other such products for those living near the Twin Towers made false claims—roughly 140,000 people.[8] A congressional study concluded that as much as $1.4 billion, nearly a quarter of the total disaster aid to victims of Hurricane Katrina, went to bogus or undeserving victims.[9] Similarly, compensation funds for victims in mass tort cases tend to attract numerous phony claims.[10]

Of course, not all of those who receive benefits that were not intended for them are bad apples. They may simply be confused. The law may be so poorly drafted or ambiguous that even a seasoned administrator, not to mention lay applicants, must guess at its meaning. For example, the term "disability" appears in numerous laws and has many different definitions. In addition, the eligibility requirements may be looser than they should be, such as granting food stamps to a college student taking a year off, who will earn big money after graduation in eighteen months. Yet even innocently or negligently false claims divert resources from the intended beneficiaries, spur the adoption of crude and often costly screening measures, weaken programs morally and politically, and may lead to reduced funding.

Because fraud and abuse in social welfare programs, and in many other government programs as well, has long been perceived as a very serious and costly public administration failure, government and civic groups routinely condemn it. Fraud and abuse is a perennial subject of audits, investigations, criminal prosecutions, and program reform, however feckless. It is often difficult to distinguish between fraud and abuse by bad apples, on the one hand, and government maladministration, on the other. Both factors, for example, may account for the fact that the Social Security Administration's disability program overpaid $990 million in 2003, an error rate that seems to be growing.[11] Similarly, some underpayment of taxes and receipt of excessive tax credits (as with the EITC) surely reflect taxpayer confusion in the face of remarkably opaque rules. In short, fraud and abuse problems receive plenty of attention. Precisely for this reason, we focus on those bad apples whose misconduct does not rise to the level of criminality, although some of our examples do include bad apples whose misconduct may also be criminal.

Bad Apples in Specific Programs

We have investigated the bad apples problem in three of the most prominent and costly social programs designed to improve the welfare and prospects of the disadvantaged: public schools, public housing, and municipal homeless shelters. However, there is every reason to believe that bad apple participants inflict similar harms in job training, drug rehabilitation, and many other social programs.

As noted in chapter 1, the data presented in these case studies are neither systematic nor rigorous and certainly not complete. Therefore, we base no strong claims on the data. Instead, we present these case studies to illustrate the nature and magnitude of the bad apples problem in cities, particularly those with embedded poverty, to highlight the need for more data on the problem in these and other programs (discussed in chapter 7), and to suggest how officials might better manage the problem in their own programs. These case studies show that within each program the bad apples problem is chronic and significant, that the existing processes for removing them may actually exacerbate the problem, that some programs are experimenting with modest, low-cost approaches to improving these processes, and that these approaches might be useful in addressing the problem in still other programs.

Public Schools

Widespread, intense concern about the harmful effects of disruptive students on their peers is evident in public opinion polls and surveys of both teachers and students.[12] This finding is hardly surprising. The externality and public good aspects of classroom education mean that just as students can learn from each other as well as from their teachers, so too can one student's misconduct quickly cascade through the classroom, thereby reducing learning for all.[13] Although disruptive behavior and discipline problems can be defined in different ways, our data distinguish among four crude categories of misconduct: disruption, nonserious violence, violence, and criminal violence.[14] According to one report, more than 77 percent of public elementary and secondary schools suffered at least one violent incident (as defined in the report) during the 1999–2000 year, and students were more likely to fear being attacked at school than being attacked when away from school.[15] Schools that reported a large number of serious discipline problems were more likely to experience violent criminal incidents, including rape, sexual battery, physical attacks, and robbery.[16] Not surprisingly, the risk of encountering violence in school is concentrated in poor areas and is greatest for economically disadvantaged students.[17] Some believe that noncriminal incidents, which are of course far more common than violent crime, are more responsible for disrupting the educational environment and making it more difficult for students to learn.[18] There are also suggestions that officials, at least in New York City, underreport violent and disruptive incidents in the public schools.[19]

In a May 2004 study, a third of the teachers surveyed said that because of student discipline problems, they had either considered leaving or knew colleagues who had left the profession.[20] Twenty percent of parents reported that discipline problems had caused them to consider moving their child to another school or that they had already done so. Nearly eight in ten teachers (78 percent) said that their school had students who should be removed and sent to alternative schools. The same percentage reported that students are quick to remind them that they have rights or that their parents can sue. A majority of teachers (55 percent) said that discipline problems were also the result of school officials' backing down in the face of assertive parents. The survey found that parents and teachers favored allowing discipline-related lawsuits only in cases where serious sanctions like expulsion are imposed and that in such cases monetary awards against schools should be barred.

Although some federal and state laws address the problem of chronic disruption by a small core group of students, most policy responses occur at the local school district or individual school level. These responses include rules at the level of the school district or school; a number of practices, such as the use of metal detectors and hallway monitors; specific modes of punishment, such as corporal punishment (especially in the South); removal of the disruptive students from the classroom; and placement of the disruptive students in alternative schools. A number of the alternative schools serving these removed students offer crisis or behavioral intervention.[21] Nevertheless, the fragmentary evidence suggests that many efforts to remove violent and chronically disruptive students fail at that task and that the removals that do occur are often not timely.[22]

A recent study by Richard Arum of the discipline problem in public schools places much of the blame on judicial decisions that broadly extended due process rights to students in public schools, as well as on an increase in related educational regulations and legislation that have constrained the authority of teachers and school administrators and often prevented them from taking prompt and effective action to curb disruptive behavior.[23] In particular, the Supreme Court's 1975 decision in *Goss* v. *Lopez*, involving students suspended for fighting in the lunchroom, extended due process rights—there, notice and an opportunity to be heard—even to students facing relatively minor school discipline, such as suspensions of ten days or less. Presumably, students facing more serious discipline, such as expulsion or transfer to alternative programs, had more extensive procedural rights.[24]

Post-*Goss* court decisions have held that the constitutionally required hearing for a short-term suspension is minimal; one commentator insists that *Goss* would be satisfied by "a three-minute due process. . . . Tell the student the charge. Give the student the opportunity to tell his/her side of the story, listen, and make a decision." [25] The *Goss* hearing need not include written notice, pre-suspension notification of parents, an opportunity for parents to tell their side of the story, time to prepare a presentation, a right to counsel, a right to offer or cross-examine witnesses, or a right to appeal the decision. Nonetheless, state law and local school board policies often provide students with additional procedural rights. Some courts, state laws, and administrative policies have extended these rights even to in-school suspensions or isolation, as well as out-of-school suspensions shorter than that involved in *Goss*. This "due process creep," as this commentator has called it, may encourage misconduct by making it much more costly for school officials to impose discipline.

The Individuals with Disabilities Education Act (IDEA), enacted in the same year as *Goss*, conferred further substantive and procedural rights on students with disabilities.[26] The statute defines disabilities to include mental retardation, hearing impairments including deafness, speech or language impairments, visual impairments including blindness, emotional disturbance, orthopedic impairments, autism, traumatic brain injury, other health impairments, specific learning disabilities, multiple disabilities, or developmental delay. Students with these disabilities need special education and related services.

Subsequent amendments to IDEA, most recently in December 2004, expanded the rights of disabled students, notably in discipline cases. Since IDEA's purpose is to mainstream special education students into the "least restrictive environment," it limits schools' ability to remove disabled students from the classroom, particularly when their misconduct stems from their disability. Although this is a noble goal, the statute has had the severe unintended side effect of inhibiting the removal of bad apples, thereby blighting the educations of vast numbers of good apple students. (As we shall see, an analogous kind of constraint has been applied to the removal of chronic lawbreakers and disrupters from public housing and homeless shelters, at least in New York City.)

IDEA does not seriously impede removals for short periods. Schools may suspend disabled students for less than ten days for whatever reason, as long as the suspension would be appropriate for similarly situated nondisabled students. Thus, short-term suspension remains an option even when the misconduct stems directly from the student's disability. For violations related to weapons, drugs, or serious bodily injury, schools can also remove a special needs child for up to forty-five days to an interim educational setting.

Under the statute, schools cannot remove a disabled student from public school for more than ten consecutive days for disruptive behavior that falls short of "serious misconduct" and that is deemed to have arisen from the student's disability. When such a situation arises, the school must conduct a "manifestation hearing" in which the parent bears the burden of proof that the disability caused the misconduct. (Until July 2005, the school bore the burden of proving that the misconduct was not disability related.) In addition, parents are statutorily entitled to a due process hearing to vindicate the child's right to a "free and appropriate" public education. Under IDEA, if the misconduct did not arise from the disability, then the school may suspend the student but must still provide an interim alternative education program that provides the instruction that the student needs to make effective progress. In addition to this federal statute, forty-one states (as of 2000) had passed laws establishing the reasons for which students can be expelled or suspended, and forty-nine had laws setting grounds for expulsion.[27]

Nevertheless, two problems remain: showing that disruption was not due to disability (which has been very broadly defined) and providing quality education to others despite the presence of disruptive students whose misbehavior is determined to be disability related. In practice, suspensions are very infrequent and expulsions exceedingly rare, despite the widespread disruptive behavior. The Department of Education provides the most comprehensive nationwide data on suspensions and expulsions based on reports from 88,000 schools for the 2000–01 school year. Of the 46,300,000 students in the database, 6.6 percent received out-of-school suspensions, and only 0.21 percent were expelled.[28] The suspension rate varied from state to state. In North Dakota, 2.4 percent of students were suspended; in South Carolina, the figure was 14.6 percent. For expulsions, the rate across states ranged from zero to just under 0.8 percent. Thus, the bad apples who are removed even temporarily appear to comprise only a small fraction of the bad apple populations within schools.

Disabled students protected by IDEA and other such laws are seldom suspended or expelled from public schools. Approximately 1.4 percent of the almost 6 million students considered disabled and receiving services under IDEA (who in turn constitute about 12 percent of all students) were removed for a period greater than ten days during 2000.[29] A Government Accountability Office (GAO) study, based primarily on a survey of middle and high school principals in a limited number of states, found that the rate of incidents of serious misconduct—violent behavior, drugs, weapons, firearms—was more than three times higher among students with disabilities than among regular education students (50 per thousand versus 15 per thousand). In both groups, 60 to 65 percent of students who engaged in serious misconduct were given out-of-school suspensions, and about one in six was expelled. The main difference was that a higher proportion of expelled special education students received postexpulsion education services.[30] In addition to the IDEA rules, many local school districts (86 percent of those responding to the GAO survey) have adopted their own protections for disabled students on top of IDEA rules; these additional protections, often imposed by court-mandated consent decrees, obviously restrict disciplinary actions even more.[31] Almost two-thirds of principals reported that they operate under a local policy that prevents them from suspending special education students for more than ten cumulative days in a school year.

We suspect, but the existing data cannot demonstrate, that disruptive students who are not disabled and thus are not covered by IDEA can nonetheless take advantage of the constraints on disciplinary action that IDEA imposes on schools. Principals surely have more difficulty expelling student A, who is not covered by IDEA, when student B, who is covered by it, committed the same or worse infraction and because of the law was not expelled. Presumably, bad apple students—those who are protected by the law and those who are not—quickly learn about such disparities through the notoriously effective grapevine that exists in schools. One would expect them, as the notion of moral hazard suggests, to take these disparities into account in deciding how to behave.

Students are increasing likely, through their parents, to challenge their school-imposed punishments in the courts. This trend, which has been facilitated by changes in the law governing school discipline that began in the 1990s, has greatly complicated the problem of school discipline. Urgent public concern about disruptive and violent students possessing and selling weapons and drugs in the public schools led many states and school districts to adopt zero-tolerance disciplinary policies, often in the form of administrative rules that authorize or require school officials to impose a specific punishment, usually expulsion or long-term suspension, for certain types of infractions. At the same time, however, Congress was enacting laws protecting disabled individuals against discrimination in public programs and was also expanding the IDEA rights of disabled students (among those most likely to misbehave) to avoid school discipline for disability-related misbehavior.

The effects of this collision between public policies such as zero tolerance that increase schools' disciplinary options and other policies that limit those options by enlarging students' rights have recently been studied by Richard Arum and his associates. They find that these policy changes, which created an ambiguous legal regime surrounding school discipline, were followed by an unprecedented upsurge in lawsuits over school discipline. In this litigation, the courts tended to uphold the schools in cases involving zero tolerance discipline but favored the students in those cases where they also claimed disability. Not surprisingly, it was the more affluent parents who were more likely to litigate these cases in the appellate courts.[32] Complaints about this new legal regime have centered on multiple and violent offenders whom the schools could not quickly remove and who therefore remained to terrorize their classmates.[33]

What happens to misbehaving students who are removed from school? According to a GAO report on special needs students, removed students' short-term placements (fewer than ten days) were primarily either in in-school suspension rooms or at home, but those students removed for more than ten days were primarily placed in alternative schools or homebound placements.[34] As amended, IDEA mandates that disabled children receive a functional behavior assessment, behavioral intervention services, and modifications designed to address the misconduct; it does not require any reintegration services to prepare removed students for a return to their traditional educational settings. Under New York City law, however, students who are released from alternative programs must be placed in mainstream schools within five days of applying, and no school can turn them away.[35] This entitlement or "right of return" helps to explain why disruptive preschoolers, who ordinarily have no entitlement to preschool education, are expelled from their programs in much higher proportions than are their disruptive elders.[36]

Unfortunately, we know less about alternative arrangements for nondisabled students. Many states and localities offer alternative educational programs for students who are expelled or suspended from school.[37] As of 2000, twenty-six states required that school districts make alternative education opportunities available to suspended or expelled students. In eighteen states, school districts had discretion to establish such programs.[38] Alternative school programs are controversial. For decades, some policymakers and educators have insisted that alternatives to the traditional school model are required to meet the needs of all students, including those with chronic behavioral problems.[39] However, critics claim that "many alternative schools are no more than holding pens for children considered to be troublemakers," where children are mistreated and denied adequate instruction.[40]

In addition, the costs of providing alternative instructional services to expelled students are substantial. The American Federation of Teachers (AFT) estimated that it cost an additional $1,750 on average for a disruptive student to attend an alternative school.[41] But the AFT also found benefits that more than offset these additional costs: "the public annually gains $14,000 in student learning time that would have been lost, $2,800 in reduced grade repetition costs, $1,750 in reduced welfare costs, and $1,500 in reduced prison costs" from such a placement.[42] The AFT determined that

—when one hour of instructional time per day is lost to disruption, the cost is $23,429 a class a year (based on the national average cost of $5,623 a pupil a year);

—for each student whom an alternative program prevents from having to repeat a grade, the cost saving is $5,623;

—the average cost to incarcerate an inmate in local jails in 1993 was $14,667 a year; and

—federal prison costs average $22,773 an inmate a year.[43]

These estimates—though obviously from an interested source—show that bad apple students inflict significant harm on good apples and on the system. Much better information is desperately needed concerning these harms. Data are also needed on the variety of alternative programs to which bad apple students can be transferred, the costs and benefits of these programs, the period of time students remain in them, the degree of success of these programs in modifying bad apple behaviors and returning the transferred students to mainstream classes, the handling of disciplinary problems arising in the alternative programs, and error rates in student classifications. Separate study is required to determine to what extent IDEA actually creates externalities that affect non-IDEA students and that jeopardize other aspects of program performance. Finally, policymakers should consider whether the procedures now being afforded to students accused of bad apple conduct before they can be removed are slower, more costly, and more onerous than actually required by due process, as defined by the courts and by considerations of fairness, accuracy, and the need to protect good apples. Some commentators, at least, think that this is the case.[44]

We tried hard to obtain existing data on some of these points from two public school systems: New York City and New Haven. These efforts were stymied by a combination of factors: concerns about the effect of disclosure on pending or future litigation against the systems, fear of adverse publicity about a politically sensitive area in which the systems are struggling to cope with very difficult challenges, and other more narrowly bureaucratic considerations.[45] Whatever the reasons for denying us access to the data, filling this particular information vacuum should be a priority for policy planners.

Public Housing

Criminal activity and ruffianism seriously impair the quality of life of a large number of public housing residents.[46] Some residents, who are already disadvantaged and disproportionately members of minority groups, live in constant fear; they are prisoners in their own homes. Two separate studies by the Department of Housing and Urban Development (HUD) and the Department of Justice compare the high crime rates in public housing with crime rates in surrounding areas (which also tend to be high). These studies confirm that criminal activity in public housing projects is a very serious problem. In 1998 an estimated 360 gun-related homicides occurred in sixty-six of the nation's hundred largest public housing authorities—an average of one such homicide per day.[47] This problem extends from smaller public housing projects to those in cities of all sizes.[48]

But gun-related homicides are only the tip of the iceberg. Data for a six-month period drawn from HUD's Public Housing Drug Elimination Program, based on a sample of 559 public housing authorities, reported 423 homicides, 1,610 rapes, 8,382 robberies, 20,776 aggravated assaults, 28,777 burglaries, and 19,254 auto thefts.[49] Although public housing accounted for less than 10 percent of the nation's housing in 1999, more than twice the surrounding communities' share of crime occurred in and around public housing.[50]

From 1990 through 1999, public housing authorities spent over $4 billion to reduce and prevent crime. As HUD acknowledges, these costs divert funds from the programs' principal mission of providing shelter for low-income families. Indeed, only one in four income-eligible families now receives this housing assistance.[51]

How much of the crime in and around public housing projects is committed by resident bad apples is unknown.[52] When these malefactors can be identified, the most straightforward remedy for the housing authority is to evict them. Unfortunately, this process is much harder and slower than one might expect, especially when evicting the bad apples means evicting family members as well, be they innocents, enablers, or fellow malefactors.

Believing that drug dealers were imposing a reign of terror on public housing and other federally assisted low-income tenants, Congress enacted the Anti-Drug Abuse Act of 1988, which as later amended mandates that public housing leases provide that "any criminal activity that threatens the health, safety or right to peaceful enjoyment of the premises by other tenants or any drug-related criminal activity on or off such premises, engaged in by a public housing tenant, any member of the tenant's household, or any guest or other person under the tenant's control, shall be cause for termination of the tenancy." President Clinton, in his 1996 State of the Union Address, vowed to enforce this mandate. The Supreme Court upheld its constitutionality in *Department of Housing and Urban Development* v. *Rucker*, even as applied to the eviction of tenants who lacked any specific knowledge of the criminal activity.[53] Earlier, the Chicago Housing Authority (CHA) sought to implement the statute through sweeps of project apartments for drugs, weapons, and illegal tenants. When the ACLU challenged the CHA's practice, more than 5,000 tenants signed a petition favoring warrantless CHA searches of the apartments, including their own, to expedite the eviction of bad apples, some of whom were hardened criminals.[54]

We investigated how the bad apples problem is handled by New York City's public housing agency, which is reputed to be among the most progressive, well-managed in the country.[55] The New York City Housing Authority (NYCHA) is the largest public housing authority in the country, with approximately 417,000 authorized residents (5.2 percent of the city's population) in 180,000 units in 345 developments consisting of almost 2,700 residential buildings, which contain more than 3,300 elevators. NYCHA residents and Section 8–voucher holders occupy 12.7 percent of the city's total rental housing stock. Almost 40 percent of the residents are younger than 21 years of age, and the vast majority are under the age of 18. The waiting list for apartments is long (145,000 families toward the end of 2005), and waits of many years are common.[56]

NYCHA officials estimate the incidence of bad apples among NYCHA residents to be quite low, perhaps 0.5 percent, yet they insist that "just a few bad apples can ruin an entire building." Sometimes, there are more than a few. For example, at one complex, Redfern Houses, the police made 27 felony arrests in one day for drug sales on the site. Drug trafficking activity had, in effect, confiscated the public areas from use by other tenants. Seniors were forced to remain inside, and children could not play on the grounds of the complex. The perpetrators filled the hallways with the stench of urine, monopolized the lobbies, broke the locks and doors, prevented legitimate residents from using the elevators, and kept the elevators out of service. Such conditions can readily create a (literally) vicious circle in which chronically disruptive tenants drive away law-abiding ones. Our discussion here focuses on bad apples in the projects who harm other tenants. But bad apples also inflict significant costs on the housing authority; thus drunkenness leads to fire damage in an apartment, and lack of personal hygiene creates infestations.[57]

Eviction of nuisance tenants who degrade the quality of life in the projects but whose behavior does not rise to the level of criminality is apparently rare. New Haven Housing Authority officials could not recall a single instance when a tenant was successfully evicted merely for being a nuisance to his or her neighbors.[58] Failure to remove a few bad apples predictably causes many good ones, at least those with any choices, to leave, making conditions for those who remain even worse. And presumably some impressionable good apples get seduced into becoming bad apples.

The process for protecting good apple residents from the bad ones, particularly in the case of drug trafficking, was initially governed by the *Escalera* decree, a 1971 settlement reached between New York City and antipoverty lawyers in a federal court case.[59] This decree created a four-stage process. First, the housing project's manager interviewed the tenant and sought to resolve the matter. If unsuccessful, the manager then submitted the file, along with his recommendation and reasons, to the tenancy administrator. Second, the tenancy administrator would review the recommendation to determine whether probable cause for eviction existed, in which case the file was then referred to the NYCHA legal department for the preparation of charges and formal notice to the tenant of a hearing. Third, the hearing officer held a hearing and rendered a written decision and recommended a proper disposition of the case. Fourth, the hearing officer's report and the tenant's reply, if any, were submitted to the housing authority board for their final review and determination of the action that should be taken. In drug-related evictions requiring a full hearing by the housing authority board, this process typically took nine months. Then, if the tenant still did not vacate, NYCHA had to commence a "holdover proceeding" to obtain a judicial warrant of eviction, which took another two to four months. The tenant could win further delay by challenging the housing authority's decision in a state trial court and then moving for a stay of the proceeding. The district attorney sometimes insisted that the NYCHA hold up on its evictions until a criminal proceeding could be brought. Ordinary criminal proceedings, where jail is the far more serious potential penalty, hardly offer alleged offenders the protections of such elaborate processes.

Finding the decree's procedures too cumbersome to enable the NYCHA to protect good apple residents from drug trafficking and other serious violations, the city's district attorney began in the late 1980s to seek to evict NYCHA tenants under the so-called Bawdy House law, which authorizes a civil court proceeding seeking summary eviction where the premises are "used . . . for any unlawful trade or manufacture, or other business."[60] In 1996 the federal court with jurisdiction over the *Escalera* decree issued a decision modifying the decree to permit NYCHA to seek evictions under this law. This change would enable it to complete many of these evictions in two to three months instead of the usual nine months. The court found that

—since the 1970s, drug-related crime and drug-related violence, including homicides, perpetrated on housing authority premises had increased enormously;

—"speedy evictions of drug-traffickers from Housing Authority apartments is an effective means of disrupting the drug market" (particularly with "new initiates"), because it ends access to apartments needed for secure and stable locations for drug sales and storage and increases neighbors' willingness to inform against drug dealers, which they are often fearful of doing;

—the delays entailed in evicting drug-trafficking tenants under the *Escalera* decree procedure were handicapping NYCHA's ability to provide decent, safe, and sanitary housing;

—residents "often must withstand home environments littered with violence and the other ills associated with the trafficking of narcotics";

—"with a nearly zero vacancy rate every apartment occupied by a drug-trafficker is one less apartment which a law-abiding applicant can possess"; and

—expedited proceedings were necessary to change the drug culture in NYCHA projects and to end the "scourge in Housing Authority communities."

In the decade since the *Escalera* decree was modified, NYCHA's officials say, the agency's use of the expedited eviction process has helped stem the tide of drug trafficking in its projects. This in turn has contributed to the stunning decline in the crime rate in the city as a whole. During this period, however, a major limitation in the usefulness of the Bawdy House law became apparent. That law only authorizes proceedings in the case of illegal "business," not in cases involving more isolated incidents or violence apart from economic gain—such as mere intimidation, turf warfare, or fighting, all common occurrences. For this reason, NYCHA could not use it to remove tenants engaged in criminal activity that did not constitute a business or enterprise. To remedy this situation, in June 2004 Mayor Michael Bloomberg announced plans for Operation Safe Housing, a streamlined and prioritized process for evicting criminal activity that the Bawdy House law did not cover, particularly the most serious sex crimes, gun violations, and drug offenses that did not constitute trafficking.

The program, inaugurated in January 2005, created a streamlined adjudication process within NYCHA and also in a special part of the city's housing court. A new chief hearing officer was assigned with the sole responsibility of hearing eviction charges against the worst apples whose offenses appeared on a specific priority list developed with the police department. Improved coordination with the police through a designated contact person for NYCHA cases accelerated the preparation of the police reports and forensic work needed to support prompt eviction, and also allowed for police officers to be available to testify at the hearing. NYCHA reorganized its internal management of the eviction process for these priority cases, with new systems for file coding, training, and utilizing its attorneys and investigators, thereby reducing the number and length of agency-caused delays.

Although Operation Safe Housing has been in effect for only a short period, one result is already clear. In the first 635 eviction cases under the new procedure, the average time from the commencement of the process to its resolution—such as actual termination of the tenancy, probation, permanent exclusion of one or more persons in the household, and lesser remedies—has been cut by more than two-thirds, from nine months to less than three months. Assuming that the *Escalera* judge was correct to find that speedy eviction of bad apples improves the safety and quality of life of good apple families in the projects, this acceleration of the process constitutes an immense gain, achieved at what appears to be modest cost and with no sacrifice of due process.[61] If these encouraging results continue, NYCHA plans to expand the program to fraud and violent crimes not now covered by Operation Safe Housing. This program represents a remarkable success. It shows that the worst of the bad apples can be removed from the projects more swiftly while maintaining procedural safeguards. And this success has been achieved in one of the most politically liberal communities in the country.

The so-called barment process represents another promising approach to removing bad apples, with a focus on those who are visitors. This can take a variety of specific forms, but its basic thrust is a policy under which the housing agency and the local police serve a formal notice on individuals who lack a legitimate business or social purpose for being on the premises. This barment notice states that they are subject to arrest for trespassing if they remain or return after having received the notice. This also subjects bad apple tenants to eviction under a lease provision prohibiting them from harboring such individuals.[62]

Homeless Shelters

The difficulty of removing bad apples from public housing applies doubly to homeless shelter programs.[63] Such removals are more difficult because the programs are the shelters of last resort, and the law prohibits them from turning away anyone who claims to need shelter—however bad an apple he may be—unless he needs to be in an acute health care facility. In addition, the availability of housing vouchers to the homeless may create a particularly perverse form of moral hazard, in which becoming homeless is a family's fastest route to getting its own apartment.[64]

The scale of New York City's shelter system is immense. On a typical night in mid-March 2006, the system for single adults provided beds to more than 8,150 individuals, served almost 1,500 more adults in drop-in centers, and made contact with 300 in the city's streets. Although the great majority of those who are sheltered use it for only a few nights, long-term users (more than nine months) account for about 20 percent of the total bed-nights. A second group, families with children, total more than 6,500 people served (representing almost 21,000 family members), and their average length of stay is much longer, about one year. A third group, childless couples, is the fastest-growing segment of the shelter population, and they also tend to remain for a long time.

Shelters have a substantial bad apples problem. The dangerous misconduct ranges from smoking in bed and creating fire risks, to alcohol and drug abuse and trafficking on the premises, to brandishing of weapons and other threatening behavior, to fighting and physical violence against both staff and fellow residents. The three main categories of bad apple behavior—what the agencies label as serious misconduct—are violence or active illegal conduct, unreasonable rejection of suitable housing, and violation of the individualized "independent living plan." All residents must negotiate such a plan with the shelter, which commits them to pursuing treatment for substance abuse, searching for available housing units, applying for entitlements, and so forth.

If the serious misconduct continues, the agency can recommend that an individual be excluded from the shelter system for a maximum of thirty days unless he or she terminates the misconduct before then. (In contrast to individuals, misbehaving families escape even this sanction. In a remarkable example of an incentive that actually *rewards* bad appledom, the only available sanction against a family is to place it in permanent housing.)

This agency recommendation for sanctions is but the first step in a very protracted, costly, and multilayered administrative process, at the conclusion of which judicial review may occur. Under a consent decree entered in an earlier case (known as *Callahan*), the agency may not impose sanctions if the individual's misconduct was "due to the physical or mental impairment of the individual or a family member," a provision that is reminiscent of IDEA protections for disruptive students.[65] A startling fact suggests that this process in effect immunizes those charged with wrongdoing, while doing nothing to protect other residents: none of the fifteen or so cases of serious misconduct for which the agency has been seeking sanctions since 2004 has yet been resolved. In mid-2006 each was still pending at the administrative or judicial level, with no end in sight.[66]

The costs of this manifestly feckless process far exceed the substantial time of staff and lawyers and the expense required to work up and pursue each case. The demoralization of shelter administrators and staff has taken its toll. Observing that months and even years go by without the imposition of any sanction even for serious misconduct, they find it increasingly difficult to take the sanctioning process seriously or to put in the substantial resources that are required to pursue what seems like a fruitless effort. But demoralized administrators are just one group that is hurt. The good apples feel that they are unprotected and may well wonder whether their self-discipline is self-defeating. The bad apples know that if the process bogs down, as it invariably does, they have won the game. Like the bad apples in public housing, they can hope to remain indefinitely.

Remedial Strategies

Once program managers properly classify people as bad apples—through processes analyzed in chapter 6—the difficult question becomes how best to deal with them. We distinguish three remedial strategies: preventing them from becoming bad apples in the first place, rehabilitating those who become bad apples despite such prevention efforts, and protecting good apples from bad ones so that the former can benefit from social policies designed for them.

Prevention

Preventing people from becoming bad apples is a compelling goal for moral reasons and to reduce a variety of social costs. Many public and private programs aim to cultivate good apples and prevent the formation of bad ones; the results of these programs, however, are mixed. Some programs appear to be somewhat successful in preventing potential bad apples from becoming such. For example, whereas school-based programs that target specific bad apple conduct, from drugs to shootings, have had little success in preventing that conduct, broad-scale programs seeking to change the schools' climate have shown promise. Such programs include those that seek to clarify norms, teach self-control, and even campaign against bullying.[67] And although there is no evidence that programs for mentoring, recreation, or advertising of crime prevention are effective in preventing serious youth violence, the Big Brothers Big Sisters mentoring program does seem to reduce substance abuse.[68] A recent research panel of the National Institutes of Health concluded that detention centers, boot camps, and other get tough programs are not only ineffective at preventing youth violence but may even worsen the problem, but the panel praised family intervention policies.[69]

The root causes of bad behavior in most instances, however, are elusive and hard to determine or change. Any sensible and humane policy must seek to identify and address root causes, but the sad truth is that social policy can seldom alter them in the short and even medium term once a child reaches a certain age.[70] Beyond that age, as we discuss immediately below, dealing with the symptoms may be all that policymakers can realistically hope to do. Even when policymakers think that they have diagnosed root causes, their programs may be poorly designed to address them, or inadequately funded, or both. Prevention programs, moreover, usually intervene only after the patterns of misbehavior by at-risk individuals are already formed and embedded, which helps to explain why so many well-intended, apparently well-designed prevention programs fail.

Rehabilitation

Rehabilitation presents no brighter a picture of policy effectiveness. For example, the results of most programs designed to reduce recidivism among prisoners and juvenile offenders are quite discouraging.[71] A comprehensive review in the early 1970s of offender treatment programs concluded that the vast majority of rehabilitative efforts had not appreciably reduced recidivism—and may have increased it.[72] Another review published in 2005 indicates that those discouraging results remain true today; recidivism rates have risen despite significant rehabilitative efforts.[73] The Department of Justice estimates that 68 percent of prisoners released in 1994 were rearrested within three years, up from 63 percent among those released in 1983.[74]

Even so, some approaches show greater promise than others. The use of drug courts, for example, has been praised as a promising strategy to prevent recidivism. That approach, which allows offenders to participate in judicially monitored substance abuse programs in exchange for reduced sentences or dismissed charges, has been shown to reduce recidivism compared with criminal justice alternatives.[75]

Protecting Good Apples

Our third-best but probably most realistic and attainable strategy is to protect the numerous good apples from the depredations of the few bad ones. This can best be done by removing bad apples from their midst. Society must continue its efforts to prevent people from becoming bad apples in the first place and to rehabilitate those who already are bad apples. Until these efforts succeed on a regular basis, however, the paramount moral and policy consideration must be to protect the good apples. Among the disadvantaged, they have the strongest possible claims on society's solicitude. Consider a tragically hard but common case—the student who torments his classmates, arguably because he suffered past abuse in his family. A just society will try to remedy the causes of his bullying behavior, but unless and until that can be accomplished, leaving him in the school rather than classifying him as a bad apple and removing him from the school is unfair to the far more numerous good apples seeking an education. It is also unfair to the society that pays the bill.

Our data from the NYCHA and the homeless shelter program in New York City reveal how difficult it has become to remove bad apples from programs. The government's remarkably cumbersome, costly, and ineffective legal procedures have left too many bad apples to linger, letting them continue to diminish the living conditions of the vast majority of those in public housing and shelters who are good apples. The national data on removals from the public schools indicate much the same discouraging pattern. The good news is that these removal procedures are now so dilatory and ineffective that, as the NYCHA reforms have shown, even relatively straightforward and inexpensive innovations make it possible to greatly accelerate the removal of bad apples. Such innovations can continue to provide due process while posing removal as a more realistic threat to bad apples.

Although removal will assuredly serve good apples' interests in learning or in living in a peaceful building or shelter, its effect on the bad apple, a concern albeit a secondary concern, is less clear. Removal will certainly stigmatize him, at least in the short run. This stigma is an inevitable consequence of society's condemnation of his behavior, but its burden may encourage him to change his bad apple ways and thus improve his life prospects. On the other hand, placing him in a separate program filled with other bad apples could conceivably harden and reinforce his antisocial habits.[76] If this separate program is well designed to help him change his ways and is adequately funded, however, he may be able to return to the mainstream program and begin to benefit from it. Typically, social programs are not designed with reformation goals in mind. Program administrators need to find the right balance between removal and second chances, in making alternative programs effective but not too attractive, and in targeting these efforts appropriately for each bad apple.

Let us be crystal clear, recalling points made in chapter 2 about what should happen to bad apples who are removed. We do not propose that society give up on them; we would not send the chronically disruptive student, public housing tenant, shelter resident, or chronic substance abuser to the equivalent of Devil's Island or a remote leper colony. Our goals, rather, are prevention, rehabilitation, and protection of others. First, one must not be classified as a bad apple without an opportunity for a hearing. If so classified one must have the right to appeal the classification immediately or to apply for an exception based on special circumstances. (See chapter 6.)

If the classification holds up, however, the program should move the bad apple to an alternative environment. In the case of chronically disruptive students, this environment will probably be one with tighter physical controls, a higher staff-to-student ratio, and more intensive counseling. (We say "probably" because we possess no specialized knowledge concerning how best to rehabilitate bad apple students, or indeed any other kind of bad apple. This is a matter for the experts in particular fields, at least in the first instance.)[77] Even then, they should always have access to services that encourage and enable them to reform, so as to eliminate the apple's rot. We recognize that separate educational programs for bad apples may be costly, perhaps even more costly than those for good apples.[78] But if this separation reduced slightly the resources spent on good apples (we have no good data on this point), the good apples could still be far better off. This would occur if the reduced disruption enabled them to benefit much more from the remaining resources being spent on their behalf. And if separation into an alternative program causes bad apples to inflict less harm on society in the future, so much the better. Our prescriptions for dealing with other bad apples removed from nonschool programs are discussed in the final section of chapter 2.

Bad apples need not always be removed from good ones. Removal is sometimes impossible and perhaps undesirable. For example, society opposes separating a typical single teenage mother from her child, family, or school unless there simply is no other viable choice. The first duty of policymakers is always to strive conscientiously to rectify bad apples' conduct. Both morality and sound policy dictate that society should not give up on them prematurely (or perhaps ever); it should instead try to help them redeem their lives. But when the harm that bad apples inflict is sufficiently great, policymakers must always seriously consider the separation option. Reforming bad apples is a commendable social goal when it can be pursued without making the good ones worse off, but this must always be secondary to the goal of protecting and benefiting the latter.

Denouncing welfare cheats, malingerers, and many other kinds of bad apples requires little political or moral courage. But actually helping the disadvantaged by changing their incentives in hopes of deterring antisocial behavior by good and bad apples alike is a much more difficult undertaking, one that generations of politicians assiduously avoided until the 1996 welfare reform. The reformers, including President Bill Clinton, many members of Congress, and some advocates for the poor, deserve much credit for squarely taking on most of the abuses of the pre-1996 welfare programs. Here, the bad apples included able-bodied adults who resisted seeking or accepting work or job training for which they were functionally capable, men and women who decided to have children whom they knew they could not adequately support, and unwed mothers who refused to work despite suitable jobs and adequate child care opportunities. Some of the reformers' customary allies vilified them; indeed, several prominent Clinton appointees resigned in protest, and social welfare scholar Daniel Patrick Moynihan, then Democratic senator from New York, dubbed the reform "the most brutal act of social policy since Reconstruction."[79]

Even now, the 1996 welfare reform remains intensely controversial. Indisputably, it has dramatically reduced welfare utilization and dependency. These caseload reductions persisted even after the economy weakened in 2001. Most recipients believe that they and their children are achieving better lives and prospects. The law's supporters note that child poverty is now below 1996 levels and that employment has increased among single-parent families. Critics, however, point out that child poverty has risen since 2001 and that the earnings plus transfers of welfare recipients have taken only a few out of poverty even after several years in the workforce. Both sides point to changes on a range of measures of child and family well-being. Program savings from declining cash assistance caseloads have been used to help the good apple poor find work, care for their children, and sustain their families; others have been forced to fend for themselves. The law appears to have reduced domestic violence in low-income families. Moreover, this has been accomplished without the dreaded outcomes for children and families that so many opponents of the reform had firmly predicted.[80] Indeed, PRWORA and the policies that followed may have contributed to the sharp reduction in out-of-wedlock births over the last decade.[81]

Protection of good apples against bad ones is also difficult because some social service professionals insist that their worst-off clients should enjoy the first claim on resources regardless of whether or not they contributed to their own misfortunes, and almost regardless of the amount of damage they inflict on better apples. Understandably, many of these professionals view themselves more as advocates for their clients than as guardians of the system's fiscal and moral integrity, and so they resist a triage process that excludes bad apples. Some of them long for a welfare state that is sufficiently generous to render such hard choices unnecessary, which they hope would reduce the need for exclusion or removal. In reality, however, failing to remove the few bad apples harms the many good ones by increasing the already formidable obstacles to progress that poverty has placed in their way.

6

Predictive Accuracy and Procedural Protection

hapters 1 and 2 briefly discussed target efficiency, which we defined as directing resources to those who can make the best use of them, while not harming others. This concept was extended and applied in our analysis of bad bets (chapter 4) and bad apples (chapter 5). In this chapter, we examine the most important methods for achieving target efficiency. We first discuss how target efficiency affects the way eligibility for social programs should be determined and which institutions should make and apply those determinations. Then we consider the two most important prerequisites for the pursuit of target efficiency: predictive accuracy in classifying people and procedures to protect them against erroneous classification.

In this analysis, we move back and forth between examples using bad apples and those using bad bets. These two categories of recipients are quite different, of course, and for many purposes must be dealt with in disparate ways. Nevertheless, for the statistically related issues analyzed in this chapter—particularly how to classify individuals into a bad bet or bad apple category and what the social and personal costs of errors are—the conceptual problems in dealing with bad bets and bad apples are quite similar. But where appropriate, and particularly in the discussion of procedural protections, we shall treat the two separately.

When Is Target Efficiency Salient?

Social programs tend to use fairly bright-line criteria to determine who will and will not be covered, for reasons of administrative ease and procedural fairness. Typically such criteria are easily measured and readily monitored, so that classification decisions are relatively straightforward. For example, all students in a certain age range may go to public school, all people below a particular income level get Medicaid, and public housing eligibility depends on income and family size. Given the limited supply of public housing relative to need, we would in theory like to monitor applicants to determine whether they could live with a relative with modest loss of utility, just as we would like to screen for students who might be better placed in private vocational training programs. But legislators have denied administrators such discretion.

Many other programs rely at least implicitly on some sort of benefit-cost consideration. For example, a state may provide that anyone with at least a C+ average in high school may enroll in a community college. Note here that it is not directing resources to those individuals who got the worst draws; they may well be the ones with lower grade point averages. Rather, policymakers think that students with better grades will benefit more from going to college. In our terms, they are more likely to be good bets. The good bets–bad bets distinction is particularly useful when established criteria predict which candidates for assistance will derive the greatest benefit. For example, job training and drug rehabilitation programs often allocate slots according to candidates' predicted likelihood of success. In contrast, a criterion based on when psychiatric visits cease to be sufficiently beneficial to justify their cost would be harder to administer. Many insurance companies simply cover a specified number of visits a year, sacrificing target efficiency to administrative ease and the desire to avoid difficult and perhaps controversial determinations.

Whatever the criteria used, a program must establish the procedures through which they will be applied. To some extent, these procedures will turn on technocratic considerations—for example, the quality and quantity of information that particular procedures will elicit, the cost of acquiring that information, and types and rates of error. But procedures also exhibit dignity and fairness aspects that, together with the technocratic ones, may raise political and legal issues. The discussion that follows touches on all of these factors.

Figure 6-1 illustrates how target efficiency ideally would work in practice. It shows three boxes in relation to eligibility. First, program administrators

Figure 6-1. *Target Efficiency Screening*

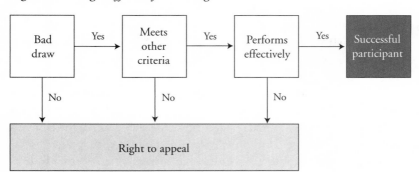

assess whether an individual received a bad draw. Second, they examine other criteria for eligibility. Merely being a bad draw does not entitle one to participate in most social programs: being disabled does not provide automatic entry to income-support programs or community college, for example. Third, program administrators apply criteria internal to their programs, such as an individual's attendance record in a job training program, to determine whether the applicant is meeting program standards. If the applicant meets all three of these tests, he is deemed a valid participant. Failure to meet any of them excludes him, although there is usually a right to appeal the exclusion. Thus the frequently absent recipient of job training might present a medical excuse.

In many social programs, only one or two of the boxes in figure 6-1 would apply. For example, a program might depend only on certain objective criteria, without requiring an applicant to prove that he has received a bad draw in life; thus a poet and part-time waiter with a Ph.D. in English would qualify for food stamps. Other programs, such as open-enrollment community colleges, use only the third box. Any high school graduate can enroll, but if her college grades are too low, then she must withdraw.

This figure emphasizes the importance of procedural fairness in targeting benefits by providing a right to appeal at every step. If an appeal is successful, the individual is restored to the time line, on the path to being a valid participant. (See figure 6-5, which includes the appeals process.) Sometimes, the program may attach conditions to this reinstatement. For example, the student asked to withdraw from college for poor grades may successfully appeal because of illness the previous semester, but the school may require that her grade point average be even higher than normal for her to continue in the program.

Will allowing appeals impede target efficiency? Program administrators have classified the current participants using appropriate criteria, and now some of those identified as bad apples or bad bets can raise objections of fact or interpretation in hopes of restoring their eligibility. But in contrast to the criminal justice system, which sometimes lets bad apples off on appeal because the police failed to follow a mandatory procedure, such as procuring a warrant or giving a Miranda warning, the process for screening applicants to determine eligibility for social programs will be much less careful and intensive at the first stage. At that stage, those identified as bad bets or bad apples will have participated minimally or not at all. In these programs, an appeals process allows a much less costly and intrusive first sorting to proceed—one that should be generally accurate but far from infallible. When a disappointed applicant claims to be the victim of an error, an appeal will adduce much more individual-specific information and correct most, if not all, errors. In effect, two sorts are cheaper and better than one. Using appeals as part of the sorting process, then, should increase the target efficiency of social programs, as we elaborate below.

Our discussion of appeals focuses on petitions by individuals claiming that they were misclassified. There would be obvious merits as well to allowing program administrators to appeal the decision to enroll an individual in a program. However, considerations of due process and fairness weigh more heavily when an individual may have been wronged; hence that is where we focus our appeals discussion.

Who Chooses?

Most of our discussion assumes that a central authority chooses the eligibility criteria and then administers whichever classification and appeals processes are in place. But there are a variety of ways to determine who gets benefits. We discuss four of them: sorting by authorities, sorting by universal programs, retrospective sorting, and sorting by recipients. Many programs employ various combinations of these mechanisms. In addition, each method has its own advantages and disadvantages. For example, administrative costs are lower in universal programs or when recipients sort themselves.

Sorting by Authorities

Figure 6-1 depicts a conventional social program. In sorting by authorities, a central authority, usually a legislature or executive agency, establishes eligibility criteria and a process for selection and review. (Although each of the three

other ways of choosing is also established by authorities, they deviate substantially from the social program in figure 6-1.) In a variant of this process,
the government sometimes delegates the eligibility-setting job to another
organization, which it believes can do a better job of determining who would
benefit most from a program. Thus the gatekeeper to admission to a public
four-year college with heavily subsidized tuition is usually the college's admissions committee, although the state legislature may weigh in on the criteria
that the committee uses. Many churches and nongovernmental organizations
run homeless shelters, each establishing its own rules for who can come, for
how long, and on what conditions. (Chapter 5 discusses how these rules are
enforced against bad apples.) Some of these shelters receive direct government funding, and all such legitimate nonprofits are eligible for tax-
deductible contributions. Thus private parties and government share the
expense of providing benefits. They also share sorting responsibilities: private
parties shape eligibility requirements subject to government regulation.[1]

Universal Programs

Public education and Medicare are important examples of universal programs. Everyone of a particular age is eligible. One cannot be excluded
because one is too dull, too disabled, too bright, or too healthy. Universal
programs can, however, impose additional hurdles, such as the financial
charges for participation in parts of Medicare. In such ways, even universal
programs can—and we argue, *should*—pursue target efficiency. To illustrate,
our discussion in chapter 5 of chronically disruptive students as bad apples
suggests that reasonable behavior in the mainstream public school classroom—normally a universal entitlement—should be a requirement for
remaining there.

Retrospective Sorting

Target efficiency may be sought through retrospective sorting. Suppose, for
example, that everyone is eligible for admission to a community college, but
remaining in the college requires a certain grade point average. Similarly, a
drug treatment program may require participants to have regular clean urine
tests as a condition for continued treatment. Two assumptions explain why
some programs rely heavily on retrospective sorting. First, policymakers
believe that the opportunity to participate should be given liberally. Second,
they cannot accurately predict how particular individuals will benefit from
the program, but they believe that performance in the program is directly
correlated with benefits, with those who perform well securing much larger
benefits from it.

Sorting by Recipients

Potential recipients can be induced to sort themselves. They already do so in many programs. Thus individuals need not participate in Medicare, and families dissatisfied with public schools can send their children to private schools or charter schools. For their part, private and charter schools can use academic standards to encourage only dedicated students and families to apply. For example, Boston's Academy of the Pacific Rim requires every student to follow an exacting academic schedule, including seven years of Mandarin. (Despite the school's name, East Asian students comprise less than 5 percent of the student body.) As a result, the Academy well outperforms the city and state on test scores.[2]

Sometimes an individual self-sorts when she decides whether to apply to a charter school, a job training workshop, or another program. At other times, applicants gain entry by adjusting their choices to the eligibility criteria. If Medicaid accepts only individuals who earn less than $12,000 per year (the 2006 limit for Medicaid beneficiaries in New York), then someone who wants to enroll must keep his earnings below that level. We discuss below two mechanisms that programs can use to induce recipients to sort themselves: fees and ordeals.

FEES. If a job training program merely asks a candidate whether he will work hard, his answer will obviously be yes, whatever may be his true intention or capacity. The program can elicit a truer signal in several ways, including the imposition of a small participation fee. The fee or imposition must be large enough so that the candidate will think hard about whether he can muster the commitment needed for success in the program and small enough to avoid excluding good bets who, through no fault of their own, cannot come up with the necessary funds. The program can minimize this last possibility by setting the fee on an income-based sliding scale, by making it refundable once the candidate has demonstrated the requisite effort in the program, or even by waiving it in appropriate circumstances. If someone is unable or unwilling to raise the fee, then he is probably a worse bet than someone who can. This system will inevitably miss the presumably rare person who can do neither but who is nonetheless genuinely committed and a good bet. Perhaps other low-cost methods can be devised to flag these unusual cases.

Fees, then, are screening devices designed to separate those who really care from those who do not, those who deserve the benefit from those who do not. Consider a dramatic, non-American example. Antimalaria sleeping nets are sometimes provided for free in Africa through various programs. A survey found that 70 percent of recipients did not use the nets if they got them for free but that almost all of those who paid for the nets used them.[3] Fees are widely used by public four-year and community colleges to help them balance their budgets. But if raising money were the colleges' sole concern, and if only good bets were enrolled, then zero tuition and more state monies would have better distributional effects. (This assumes that the criterion for distributional benefit is current income (the normal measure), rather than projected future income (a possibly more desirable measure.)

ORDEALS. As we discussed in chapter 4, many social programs attempt to screen out recipients who are bad bets because their prospects are too *good*. Society may not want a Ph.D. poet, who could easily get a teaching job and whose parents have significant assets, to secure benefits, such as food stamps, that are intended for bad draws with few earning opportunities, whatever the regulations may say. A typical solution to this screening problem is to have the program impose nonmonetary costs to participate; such ordeals induce recipients to reveal their true preferences and needs.[4] If one must wait in line for hours to get food stamps or participate in a public employment program to get cash benefits, the Ph.D. poet will have a strong incentive not to participate, whereas the individual with few prospects will have no choice. To be sure, ordeals impose deadweight losses, but their ability to improve target efficiency by eliciting valuable information has made them a component of many social programs. A more self-conscious consideration of this mechanism, rather than mere implicit acceptance of ordeals when they happen to arise, could make them more useful policy instruments. No doubt some uses would be curtailed and others expanded.

In considering whether these information-eliciting fees and ordeals are just, recall that in nonentitlement (discretionary) programs, even the neediest, most deserving applicant has no ex ante right to participate. Such strategies are irrelevant, however, when the benefit is an entitlement for which all who meet the statutory criteria automatically qualify, such as Medicaid, food stamps, or the EITC. In such cases, the government is obliged to fund the benefits without any explicit rationing. (We say explicit rationing because even entitlement programs, such as Medicaid, find ways to reduce costs and prioritize benefits.) In entitlement programs, recipients can enjoy the benefits passively; their inability to signal effort or commitment (beyond that needed to navigate the often demanding application process) will not affect their eligibility.

But most social programs are at least somewhat discretionary—for example, public housing and job training. The budgets of even the most politically successful discretionary programs, such as Head Start, are almost always pitifully limited when compared with the need and the number of eligible (although nonentitled) candidates for benefits. Accordingly, such programs must minimize the number of bad bets consuming their scarce resources. So long as a program cannot accept all good bet applicants, there is no injustice in seeking to maximize the chances that all who are selected are in fact good bets. In such cases, eliciting information from applicants is often a good way to sort. Indeed, it would be unwise not to use such information and unjust not to sort. Some will call this "creaming," but this pejorative term is an odd way to describe an effort to identify those who will benefit most from a program. Like the rhetorical accusation of "blaming the victim," which we discuss in chapters 5 and 7, the charge of creaming avoids the tough resource allocation issue and obscures its implications for individual and social justice.

Before proceeding with the task of determining who should be included in and excluded from a particular program, we should note the micro-orientation of this analysis. We do not give examples of which programs should operate and which should not, although as we make clear throughout, many of the same considerations discussed below would apply to this question. Thus a program with many bad bets or bad apples should be closely scrutinized and possibly terminated, whereas a program filled with good bets and good apples should be welcomed and possibly expanded. For present purposes, however, we focus on the determination of who participates in a given social program.

Predictions and Sorting

Making accurate predictions and classifications with respect to bad apples and bad bets is undoubtedly difficult. Nonetheless, the government often makes such determinations. For example, it decides who shall receive loans to build subsidized housing and which toxic waste sites shall be cleaned up first. The kernel of the task in such cases is to reduce the two prime types of predictive errors, namely identifying someone as a bad bet or bad apple when he is not (false positives, or Type I errors) or failing to conclude that a bad bet or bad apple is such (false negatives, or Type II errors). (The terminology comes from statistical decision theory.) That such errors cannot be eliminated entirely does not excuse policymakers from the duty to pursue target efficiency as best they can—specifically by addressing these prediction tasks directly and reducing the bad bets and bad apples problems to the extent possible.

There is one apparent qualification to this rule. Sometimes the costs of screening and analysis make prediction and sorting too expensive to be worthwhile. Guido Calabresi has described this general phenomenon, including its nonmonetary burdens, as "the cost of costing."[5] For example, a generally valuable medication might be found to offer lesser benefits for patients suffering from a particular condition that can only be ascertained through costly testing and delay. It may be cost-effective to skip further screening and give the medication to all eligible patients. However, this too is consistent with our analysis; it is simply classifying treatment strategies rather than classifying recipients as good and bad bets.

The remainder of this section discusses the struggle involved in determining who is likely to be a bad bet or a bad apple. Mistakes in classification are costly but so too are painstaking assessments. An effective system will minimize the sum of these costs. In what follows, we consider two polar approaches. The individualized information approach entails a comprehensive analysis of each potential recipient, while the simple-criteria approach classifies individuals by using a relatively small set of usually easily measurable factors. Because we believe that neither approach is satisfactory, we propose a third.

Predicting from Individualized Information

If cost were no object, a thorough investigation of each individual would offer the best method for identifying bad bets and bad apples. This is the approach taken in the criminal justice system, where prosecutors and defense attorneys gather every possible scrap of information in building a case. Given the high stakes involved in such cases, this approach makes sense.

However, for many social programs, the balance between costs and benefits swings the other way. In the case of patients hoping for heart valve replacements, for example, the individualized information strategy would raise the hopes of many who are unlikely to receive replacements, while subjecting them to time and hassle costs. Just as job applicants do not want to be called for an interview when their prospects are poor, someone with heart failure does not want to be run through a battery of tests when there is only a 1 percent chance that she will be recommended for an expensive treatment that may yield only modest benefit. This point also applies to the investigation of bad apples. A student whose past bad behavior makes him almost certain to be sent to an alternative school may not want to invoke an unpleasant appeals process, during which his past sins will be rehashed at length, just to pursue that small chance to stay in his current school.

What is more, the individualized information approach is not always practicable. Program administrators do not always have access to personal records that are strongly predictive of future experience, and some of what is available may be unusable because of privacy or legitimacy concerns. Consequently, in most cases, classification must rely at least in part on statistical prediction, often drawing from the experience of others who were once in similar circumstances.

Extrapolation on the basis of inconclusive information causes some unease, yet we rely on such imperfect statistical measures implicitly in our daily lives, often drawing on our own limited experiences. For example, we do not go back to a restaurant that has disappointed us, even though we know that even the best restaurants sometimes disappoint. We do not promote the salesman who missed a big sale, even though we know that the customer may have behaved badly. We admit students to college on the basis of SAT scores and high school grades, even though we know that the former are imperfect indicators and that the latter are inflated and inconsistently awarded within and across schools. In such cases, decisionmakers are doing the best they can with limited information. In the same spirit, doctors prescribe treatments for individuals, including often dangerous procedures such as heart valve transplants, when their best predictions, based on personal experience or the medical literature, indicate that the patient will be helped.

Predicting on the Basis of Simple Criteria

At the other end of the spectrum, decisionmakers may rely on a single criterion, or a small number of rules, in predicting who will and who will not benefit from a program. For example, recidivism may provide a useful marker of bad betdom or bad appledom or both. Experience suggests that with substance abuse, history repeats itself: if given another chance in an expensive new treatment program, few abusers who have already dropped out of multiple programs will beat the odds and succeed. Similarly, it may not pay to perform costly operations on those whose misbehavior has required numerous rehospitalizations or to spend limited rehabilitation dollars on criminals with long rap sheets. Although promoting moral redemption is certainly a worthy social goal, recidivism can powerfully predict the future behavior of criminals, substance abusers, chronically disruptive tenants, repeat dropouts, and others. In addition, it has two other benefits as a classification tool: its legitimacy is widely accepted, and its predictive accuracy increases swiftly with the repeat occurrence of low-probability events.[6] To illustrate the latter, a one-time teenage mother may be thought of as unfortunate. A two-time teenage mother falls strongly into the self-spoiler class and, as a group-stigmatizer, also hurts others.

Of course, past experience is not the only source of simple criteria. In the case of heart valve replacements, for example, this approach might impose an age cutoff for replacements at age 90. However, many criteria perform significantly less well than recidivism in predicting outcomes, which increases the potential for errors in classification. Some 92-year-olds with leaky valves would gain significant quality-adjusted life years (QALYs) from the surgery, and many 82-year-olds in relatively poor condition would reap negative QALYs because even a successful operation can produce complications that diminish a patient's vitality, especially if his condition is already weakened, or even hasten his death. Thus the age cutoff would misclassify these individuals because other factors affecting their medical conditions need attention as well.

One could always refine the simple-criteria approach—in this instance by obtaining an overall measurement of physical health, such as assessments of lung and kidney function and mobility, among others. But even then, the process would leave out other factors that are likely to affect a recipient's outcome. For example, an individual's preferences regarding end-of-life treatment could also make her a better or worse bet for surgery. The logic of this "creeping criteria" process ultimately leads to a detailed investigation of each potential recipient.

Errors of Exclusion and Inclusion

Before we present our preferred approach, it is worth taking a moment to lay out more precisely the task that decisionmakers face. The challenge of effective targeting is to determine who is a bad bet, a bad apple, or both, and who is not. Statistical analyses ordinarily begin with a null hypothesis and an alternative hypothesis and then gather evidence to see if the null hypothesis can be rejected in favor of the alternative. In our framework, the null hypothesis is that an otherwise eligible individual should be included as a recipient in a social program. The alternative hypothesis is that the individual is a bad apple or a bad bet worthy of exclusion. The evidence used to test these hypotheses can include current and past behavior, as well as factors that lie beyond an individual's control. For example, if a student severely disrupts a class, school administrators might examine his past record. If his record is clean, he almost certainly will not be classified as a bad apple. But if this disruption turns out to be his fourth offense since the beginning of the semester, the classification will probably go the other way. A 50-year-old candidate for a heart valve replacement might initially be classified as a good bet. But if he shows poor lung and kidney function, this evidence might tip him into the bad bet category.

How should we gauge the reliability of such assessments? We take as our initial benchmark the classifications that a program manager would make after extremely detailed investigations relying on individualized information.

Table 6-1. *Type I and Type II Errors, Definitions, and Examples*[a]

		Recipient category with detailed investigation	
		Good	Bad
Determination in practice	Good	Accurate classification (low-risk student stays in school) [patient gets appropriate procedure]	Type II error (high-risk student stays in school) [patient gets procedure offering low value]
	Bad	Type I error (low-risk student dismissed) [patient denied procedure offering high value]	Accurate classification (high-risk student dismissed) [patient denied low value procedure]

a. Text in parentheses is a bad apples example. Text in brackets is a bad bets example.

These are presumably the most accurate assessments. If we then reduce the number or the complexity of the criteria used, say, because of cost concerns, some of our determinations will be wrong relative to this benchmark.

Earlier, we discussed Type I and Type II errors. Table 6-1 illustrates these two types of errors, as well as the two types of accurate classifications. Whenever resource constraints prevent an investigation of individualized information, any set of reduced (or cruder) criteria will produce Type I and Type II errors. A simple way to reduce either type of error, without changing the degree of individualization of information sought, is to change the cutoff for classification. For example, if the decisionmaker sets the cutoff for bad apples at one previous infraction in the semester rather than three, she will keep many fewer high-risk students in school, reducing the Type II error rate. Yet any such gain comes at a cost: Type I errors will increase, and some low-risk students will be mistakenly removed. If she changes the cutoff to four infractions, she will keep more low-risk students but also many more who are at high risk of causing further disruption. How should she decide where to draw the line?

Figure 6-2 presents the possible outcomes in terms of combinations of Type I and Type II errors. Consider curve AA. It shows the tradeoffs between the two types of errors, assuming that a basic set of criteria is employed. Note the shape of curve AA. As the number of Type I errors falls, the number of Type II errors rises, and vice versa. Consequently, a decisionmaker reducing Type I errors should first eliminate the ones that come at the least cost in terms of additional Type II errors.

Let us assume that the decisionmaker has settled on the basic set of criteria but does not know where she wants the program to be on curve AA. Her

Figure 6-2. *Tradeoffs between Classification Errors*

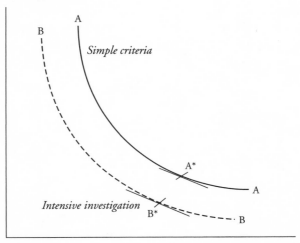

choice will depend on the relative cost of the two types of errors. When an error type is judged more expensive, the system should adjust eligibility standards to reduce it, recognizing that this adjustment generates some direct resource costs and increases the occurrence of the other error type.

For example, if keeping a genuinely disruptive student in the classroom (Type II error) is merely more hassle for the teacher, then the cost of misclassifying him as a good apple may be small. (Recall from chapter 5, however, that this hassle is a major cause of teacher dissatisfaction, burnout, and turnover.) But if the disruption significantly reduces learning by other students, the cost will be correspondingly high. An equivalent calculation applies to Type I errors. If a student who only occasionally disrupts class will learn nearly as well in an alternative school, then the cost of misclassifying him as a bad apple is small. If instead he will quickly get discouraged at the alternative school, acquire bad habits, and learn little, then the cost is high.

The second curve in the figure, BB, shows the error tradeoffs when using a larger, more refined set of criteria and a much more intensive quest for individualized information. Points A* and B* represent the optima on the AA and BB curves, respectively, if we assume that a Type II error costs twice as much as a Type I error.[7] The approach represented by curve BB makes fewer errors of either kind, but the diagnostic gain may not be worth the extra cost.

Figure 6-3. *Tradeoffs between Classification Errors Given an Appeals Process*

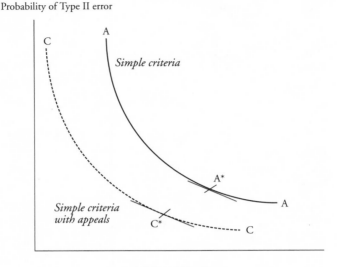

Probability of Type II error

Probability of Type I error

How should analysts choose between predicting on the basis of simple criteria (AA) and predicting from individualized information (BB)? Ideally they would compare the cost of going from AA to BB with the benefits of making fewer errors of both kinds. Or in the absence of such detailed information, they may rely on common-sense rules, such as the principle that greater investigative expenditures are justified when the stakes are higher.

Appeals and the Costs of Errors

Fortunately, we can do better than either curve AA or curve BB, quite possibly at little additional cost beyond that entailed by AA, while simultaneously affording procedural protections that society, and perhaps the law, demands.

The heart of our argument is that an appropriate appeals process can improve on curve AA without going all the way to intensive investigation of each case (curve BB, shown only in figure 6-2). This improvement is shown as curve CC in figure 6-3. The approach represented by curve CC produces fewer Type I and Type II errors, and because it involves only a small percentage of the applicants (relatively few of them appeal), it is much less expensive than the detailed investigation approach illustrated by curve BB. The preferred point on CC is at C*, assuming Type II errors are twice as costly as Type I errors.

How should an evaluation and appeals process be structured to reach curve CC and thereby reduce Type I and Type II errors? The basic principle is essentially to do a rough-sort first classification and then to allow people who think they were misclassified as bad bets or bad apples to appeal. (Presumably, only a small percentage of people will think this.) Upon appeal, they would receive a much more detailed investigation. If such an investigation is significantly more costly for bad bets and bad apples than for good bets and good apples, then only people with a strong case for reclassification will appeal. In other words, the potential participants will do much of the sorting themselves for the program at minimal cost. This system would perform even better if there were a tilt toward denial. Because those unjustly denied are more likely to appeal and those unjustly entitled surely will not, this tilt helps get the recipients to do the sorting. However, procedural fairness demands an evenhanded sorting at the first stage.

A system with an appeals process will generate far lower error and operation costs than might be expected, since so much is learned on the cheap from the recipients themselves. This happy synergy between appellate protections and more accurate prediction provides the cornerstone of an effective approach to achieving target efficiency in social programs.

Heterogeneity within Type I and Type II Errors

Anyone who is inappropriately denied participation in a program is a Type I error, a costly and unjust denial. But some unjust denials are more costly than others. Similarly, Type II errors, unmerited inclusions, differ in their cost. Given such heterogeneity, merely trading off Type I and Type II errors is not sufficient; sound decisionmaking requires a more nuanced treatment.

Suppose that we use a simple, objective criterion to decide who should be classified as a bad apple or bad bet. When the criterion produces an error, the error is likely to affect someone who is close to the cutoff line. If so, the error will be much less costly, on average, than the classification errors made by a hypothetical program administrator who merely flips a coin to decide whether applicants should be admitted to a program. Consider a hypothetical situation in which a true list of deserving heart valve recipients exists, but the medical system occasionally loses some names, and no appeal is permitted. Under these circumstances, the individuals inadvertently dropped from the list will include prime candidates for valve replacement, as well as marginally good bets. Call these lost names random Type I errors.

Now compare this system to one that uses a simple objective criterion (age) to classify individuals as good or bad bets. This approach will exclude some candidates who might be reclassified as deserving if more refined criteria were employed—for example, a robust 90-year-old. Similarly, reliance on simple criteria might lead a disruptive student with two prior infractions to be classified as a bad apple, even though a more thorough investigation might reveal that he was merely a passive follower in each case and thus deserves a second chance. Denying the robust 90-year-old a valve replacement or expelling the borderline student would be costly, to be sure, but less costly than if a coin flip determined who would receive the benefits available in each case. Thus the curves relating Type I and Type II errors in figure 6-2 are too simply drawn. Ideally, we should classify each type of error more finely—at least as low cost, moderate cost, and high cost.

Losses to Sorting: Bad Apples and Bad Bets

Sorting that uses simple objective criteria produces more errors than does sorting using more refined criteria. These extra errors are disproportionately of the low-cost kind. (We have all read about egregious cases of recidivist criminals being left in or returned to the community and of perfectly innocent people being imprisoned because of mistaken identity.[8] But these are extreme cases, which probably explains why they made the papers.) However, it is important to note that the costs these errors impose are not the same for bad bets and bad apples.

Assume that there is some true underlying scale of desirability that can be used to classify individuals as good bets or good apples; the scale goes from 0 to 100 (with higher being better), and the cutoff point is 50 for each type of applicant. Clearly, errors are costlier when misclassification occurs at the extremes: for example, a true 92 is deemed a bad apple or a true 15 a good bet. The earlier discussion of error heterogeneity, however, noted that most errors will apply to individuals close to the cutoff who were simply misgraded by a small amount.

If individuals are erroneously labeled good when they are barely bad (Type II error) and therefore incorrectly included in a program, the costs to society are qualitatively comparable, be they bad apples or bad bets. Such individuals benefit improperly, but the net social loss is probably modest if their scores are close to the cutoff.

For close cases, however, the costs of erroneous denial (Type I error) are higher for misclassified good apples than they are for those who are wrongly labeled bad bets. If an individual is classified incorrectly as a bad apple, he can claim to have been wrongly treated even if he is very close to actually being a bad apple. (For the equivalent in the criminal justice system, think of a criminal who committed a closely related crime but not the one for which he was convicted.) From a pure benefit-cost standpoint, society may be

Table 6-2. *Losses Due to Erroneous Denial of Participation*

	Bad apples	*Bad bets*
Example	Disruptive student to alternative school	Older person not given heart valve
Due process loss	Large	Modest
Utility loss	Modest	Modest in expectation, but possibly large

almost indifferent as to how this person is classified because he is so close to the line, but it will perceive any denial of due process as unfair. Indeed, this perception of injustice will persist even if the error actually costs the applicant little—if, for example, the removed disruptive student finds the alternative school nearly as good as or even better than the one from which he was removed.

Errors about bad bets, however, are quite different. Here, the parallel to the criminal justice principle of innocent until proven guilty does not apply. Bad bets have not misbehaved; indeed, most are probably exemplary citizens. However, one who is narrowly but erroneously denied a benefit may bear a nontrivial cost, such as the opportunity to receive medical treatment at Medicare's expense. What is more, errors concerning bad bets are less likely to be corrected. A patient denied a procedure is seldom well-informed and thus is less likely to appeal. Her doctor may say that given her condition, she is not a good candidate for a heart valve replacement. However, the doctor is unlikely to say that the patient would have qualified were she a year younger and her kidney function 3 percent higher. Whether such opacity reduces the patient's anxiety at the expense of her autonomy is a complicated question, analogous to similar issues that arise in the context of informed consent.[9]

Contrast the bad apple's situation. Disruptive students, we imagine, have a much better understanding of the criteria for being moved to an alternative school, and thus they will appeal when they think their case is a close one and they prefer not to move.

The relative losses of due process and utility from Type 1 errors are summarized in table 6-2. The elderly woman denied coverage was treated fairly under the standard criteria, even though a more detailed investigation would have shown that she was actually a good bet for treatment. Nonetheless, she may have suffered a significant welfare loss. In contrast, the disruptive student, who was transferred without due process to an alternative school, may have lost little in utility, depending on the stigma and his experience in the new school, even though a more thorough assessment would have revealed that this punishment was excessive. In brief, in comparison with bad bets, bad apples—in some sense being closer to the criminal justice system— receive more protection from due process, even when they may have less at stake.

Improving the System

Getting tradeoffs right between Type I and Type II errors is only one step in improving targeting through more accurate classification. Other important measures include gathering and processing more data more efficiently, anticipating strategic behavior by potential recipients, and learning from how markets handle analogous problems.

Strengthening Data Collection

If society is determined to screen more effectively for bad apples and bad bets, it must significantly improve its database. For example, policymakers interested in removing bad apples from public schools should draw on data from many school systems to ascertain the likelihood that students with various types of infractions will be chronic disrupters. Unfortunately, reliable predictors of such behavior have not yet been developed, and obtaining the data needed to develop such predictors may be difficult, as we found when officials in New York and New Haven were unwilling to give us data on their bad apples problems.

The bad bets category also needs better data. For example, although millions of individuals receive billions of medical procedures each year in the United States, virtually no systematic mechanisms integrate the results of that clinical experience. Increased use of observational studies, which look back in time at how people of various ages and physical conditions fared with heart valve replacements, for example, is one way to address this problem. Observational studies are much less costly than randomized controlled trials; they also avoid many of the ethical concerns that such trials arouse. Although less sound in statistical design, such retrospective studies have the great compensating advantage of exploiting dramatically more data. The trends toward greater reliance on electronic medical records and the practice of evidence-based medicine will facilitate observational studies; major initiatives in that direction appear to be in the offing.[10]

Equivalent data are needed to address the bad bets problem in education. For example, policymakers need to know how much members of various groups gain from going to college, which elementary school children benefit the most from enriched learning programs, the quality and cost of such programs, and so forth. Those who run individual programs have little incentive to gather such data. Moreover, the environment of competitive cream-skimming in which they operate discourages them from sharing the data they already have. Nevertheless, the dramatic reduction in the costs of accumulating, storing, transmitting, and processing information justifies much more intensive data analysis efforts. Better data would reduce both types of classification errors and significantly improve the accuracy of efforts to sort good apples from bad apples and good bets from bad bets. (In figure 6-2, the frontiers of possible error probabilities would shrink toward the origin.)

Ongoing data collection efforts are also needed to keep up with a constantly changing policy environment. For example, today's 80- and 90-year-olds are healthier on average than their counterparts of 30 years ago and constitute a much larger proportion of their birth cohort. Also, their better health status makes them, on average, better candidates for various medical procedures. Similarly, social behavior patterns, such as the incidence of fraud, shift substantially over time with new technologies and opportunities.

At the same time, however, it is important to note that data collection and processing can impose harms on dignity and privacy, in addition to financial costs. These considerations argue for setting an upper bound to the amount of individualized data that can be collected, as well as limiting efforts to combine different data sets.

Anticipating Efforts to Game the System

To enhance target efficiency, policymakers should also anticipate that applicants will try to exploit the incentives created by any classification system. Officials structure programs to elicit eligibility information from applicants. But applicants play their own strategic game in response, seeking to behave in ways that simulate the patterns that desirable applicants would display. Earlier discussion simplistically assumed that the classification system simply encounters individuals who have particular characteristics and then sorts them. In fact, we expect individuals to alter their behavior to gain eligibility, if they can do so cheaply. In chapter 3, we analyzed various forms of this behavioral response as moral hazard.

Yet potential bad apples or bad bets seeking to increase their chances of receiving social benefits may also improve their behavior. This socially desirable behavioral change, which we call *response uplift*, is the opposite of moral hazard. Our familiar bad apple, the disruptive student, may behave better— that is, just well enough to fall above the cutoff—to avoid being sent to an alternative school. Students facing the risk of failure may work just hard enough to get a grade of D. (Similarly, in markets, eggs tend to cluster in weight just above the levels required to be graded an A or a B.) From a social policy perspective, it matters not whether a potential bad apple who reforms just to avoid a penalty is really a bad apple at heart. If the behavior change is long term, the incentives to gain and retain eligibility will have worked a kind of social alchemy, turning bad apples into good ones.

Bad bets may also engage in response uplift or moral hazard. Medical procedures that require patients to be in fairly good physical condition create incentives for better behavior. But in other cases, patients only qualify for a procedure by falling *below* a certain mark, creating a perverse incentive for strategic underperformance. If healthier patients have to wait a few years for a kidney transplant, they may be tempted to abandon their prescribed diets in the hope of moving up the priority list. In the education field, a parent who wants extra tutoring for her child may discover that to be eligible, the child must read or test below a certain level or be diagnosed with a disability that will qualify her for a special education program.[11] Medicaid, public housing, and various job training programs, which target people with limited earnings, link eligibility to income. These criteria create moral hazard by providing an incentive for potential recipients to keep their incomes (or at least their on-the-books incomes) just below the eligibility cutoff. One way to minimize this risk is to impose mandatory time limits on the benefit, such as access to public housing or Section 8 vouchers, so that recipients know that they will have to return to the market and will therefore have a greater incentive to save and to develop marketable skills.[12]

In theory, more detailed investigation could reveal whether a potential bad apple or bad bet had changed behavior strategically to become eligible for a program. For example, educational administrators might compare how well a student reads in class with his performance on the entry test for a one-on-one tutoring program, which his parents may have told him to flunk. But a better strategy is for policy planners to determine ex ante which behavioral changes particular selection criteria are likely to induce. They should then design programs to induce response uplift and reduce moral hazard.

Figure 6-4 shows graphically how eligibility criteria can affect behavior. The top half, to simplify, assumes that the program uses only a minimum criterion—a threshold that applicants must reach—to determine eligibility. Many policies take this approach, such as those designed to grant admission to a heavily subsidized higher education institution. Such programs push recipients in the right direction; they elicit response uplift by encouraging individuals who might be close to the cutoff to improve their performance. The EITC is a splendid example: it gives individuals in particular income ranges larger transfers if they earn more money.[13] The 1996 welfare reform put in place a panoply of such incentives to induce recipients to better their

Figure 6-4. *The Performance Effects of Minimum and Maximum Thresholds*

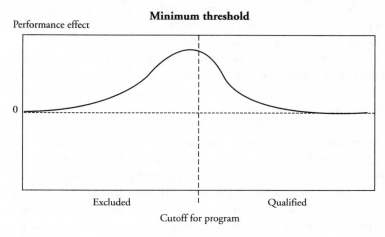

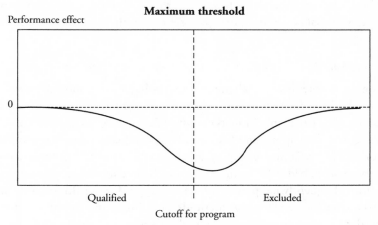

behavior. As a consequence, many former welfare recipients have gone to work, raising their incomes and reducing program costs.

The bottom half of the diagram shows programs with maximum performance cutoffs, which tend to depress the performance of individuals who might be close to the cutoff point. This happens with potential Medicaid beneficiaries who may decide to sacrifice some income to qualify for a very valuable benefit.

These cutoffs affect behavior over a distance from the cutoff point. That is because individuals do not know where their precise performance level will be, they may not know precisely what the cutoff point is, and they may suspect that the program's classification system contains some "noise." Thus even if one has qualified for a minimum performance program, one may still attempt to build in a cushion, just as students merely seeking to pass a pass-fail course frequently exceed that threshold.

Specific behavioral changes are often hard to predict. The three-strikes rule adopted by some states, which automatically imposes longer sentences on individuals convicted of two previous crimes, illustrates this difficulty. Such laws seek to incarcerate truly dangerous criminals, as three-time convicts are assumed to be. They also seek to deter individuals from becoming career criminals by upping the ante for people who have already been convicted twice. In California, which pioneered this approach, the number of three-time convicts has declined significantly. Experts believe, however, that much of this decline is because twice-convicted individuals have moved to other states where the California crimes do not matter.[14] Although an export-your-problems strategy is familiar in welfare policy, where some states have provided long-term recipients bus tickets to distant locales, California's policymakers probably did not anticipate such a result when they passed their law.

Learning from How Markets Deal with Bad Apples and Bad Bets

Screening problems are challenging, and policymakers should learn from others who have dealt with them. Particularly instructive is the experience of innumerable participants in markets who must screen out the private sector equivalents of bad apples and bad bets. For example, employers try to screen out or get rid of disruptive employees, and credit card and insurance companies try to avoid bad risks. In markets, as with government programs, predictive efforts frequently fall prey to Type I and Type II errors. In response, market participants use statistical methods to estimate the two types of costs when deciding whom to accept and whom to reject, whether for employment or for credit. Social policymakers may scale such costs differently and may be constrained by due process requirements, but taxpayers and recipients are entitled to expect that officials will screen out bad apples and bad bets when they can, with reasonable accuracy, while meeting legally required procedural fairness.

Consider some market analogies to the bad apples problem. A restaurant seeks to preserve an elegant tone by excluding diners in T-shirts or blue jeans or those who appear tipsy. A college is prepared to forgo some revenue by rejecting students who it thinks will be failures inside or outside the classroom. These are not seriously bad apples, equivalent to those we discussed in social programs, yet service providers in the market seek to exclude them because they create negative externalities. In most cases, excluding them up front will be much cheaper than removing them later—for example, flunking them out of school or expelling them from the restaurant. Hence, exclusion up front is a frequent market solution.

Bad bets in markets do not ordinarily create negative externalities, but serving them entails other costs. In this context, most bad bets are individuals who use significantly more resources than others receiving the same service or who cost significantly more to serve than the seller can charge. (Most goods are produced for an anonymous buyer, so their cost rarely depends on the purchaser's identity.) In general, market sellers have three primary ways to deal with people whom they can identify in advance as bad bets: exclude them, charge them more, or implement variable pricing.

For example, under Medicare's system of diagnosis-related groups (DRGs), the government pays hospitals a fixed amount to treat a patient with a particular diagnosis. Within diagnostic categories, however, some cases are much more complicated and costly to treat than are others, so some providers seek to exclude expensive cases from their patient mix. In insurance markets, the bad bets problem is posed by high-risk individuals, who are disproportionately likely to insure at any given premium. Insurers seek to avoid such adverse selection by ferreting out high risks and either rejecting them or charging them more. Similarly, carpenters and painters try to predict which customers are so fussy or easily dissatisfied that they will impose extra production or reputational costs. Tradesmen may turn down business from these customers, set a higher price for a job for them, or charge them on a time-and-materials basis.

By observing such strategies, policymakers may come up with better solutions to their own bad bets and bad apples problems. In addition, they can sometimes exploit information provided by markets to predict more accurately who is likely to be a bad bet or bad apple. Government-provided insurance—which extends from insurance against floods and terrorism to pensions and mortgage guarantees—provides an important example. Because of their incentives, technology, and experience, private insurers are often better at predicting the incidence of undesirable and costly events, such as accidents, illnesses, default, and fraud. Policymakers could capitalize and piggyback on these capabilities to correct their pricing of an insurance product, possibly by pricing it differentially depending on risk. To achieve this goal, the government could let private insurance companies bid to participate in a small way in any of the government's own insurance sales and then use the resulting private market price—in dollars per unit of coverage—as a guide for setting its own price. Where private intermediaries participate in government insurance transactions—for example, banks lending money for government-insured mortgages or student loans—the intermediaries could be required to bear some of the risk of default for the loans they write. This risk-sharing approach is followed by the Small Business Administration in issuing loans to businesses but virtually not at all by federal programs that back student loans.[15]

Predictions derived from market evidence can also be used to exclude broad classes of bad bets. (Bad apples need more procedural safeguards, as we explain below.) If the government is planning to protect infrastructure from terrorism, every community and facility has an incentive to qualify for the pork barrel benefits that go along with protective benefits.[16] Signals from insurance markets—notably prices, which can show policymakers which nuclear or liquefied natural gas facilities are most vulnerable and which are less so—may reduce the risk of misallocation of scarce government funds. Well-designed futures markets can sometimes help refine predictions, permitting more accurate probability assessments. Election futures, for example, have predicted recent electoral outcomes more accurately than public opinion pollsters, and futures markets are now being used in a wide range of novel applications.[17]

The law, of course, often constrains the types of exclusions that markets can employ. For example, a landlord cannot categorically refuse to rent to protected minorities even if his other tenants would pay higher rents if the minorities were excluded, and even if minority status predicted certain undesirable traits. Public officials are subject to many more strictures than private actors, including the duty to provide due process to disappointed applicants even when exclusion is permissible. Consequently, we now take up the issue of procedural protections when bad bet and bad apple classifications are being made.

Procedural Protections

The strategies discussed above can greatly improve target efficiency by improving predictive accuracy and reducing costs, but errors are almost inevitable; hence the importance of procedural protections. Certain procedures must be established to reduce the incidence of Type I and Type II errors and the costs they impose as well as to provide the safeguards for individual rights that society demands. This is particularly true in cases involving bad apples. Denying program benefits to legally eligible participants because officials deem them bad apples creates a risk of grave injustice and subsequent disadvantage to those who are erroneously classified. (As chapter 5 shows, the stakes are also high for the vast majority of participants, those properly classified as good apples.) In contrast, when it comes to bad bets, professional expertise and norms play a larger role in the classification process; there is little or no risk of moral stigma in being so classified; and the costs to good bets who might be denied service incorrectly are low in expectation, although possibly high in particular instances.

The idea that procedural protections may appropriately vary from case to case finds support in the many rulings by the U.S. Supreme Court that due process is a flexible concept and that the nature and extent of constitutionally mandated procedural rights depend on the context. In the leading case of *Mathews* v. *Eldridge*, the Court held that a utilitarian calculus determines the specific procedures required by due process, involving the interaction of "three distinct factors: first, the private interest that will be affected by the official action; second, the risk of an erroneous deprivation of such interest through the procedures used, and the probable value, if any, of additional or substitute procedural safeguards; and third, the Government's interest, including the function involved and the fiscal and administrative burdens that the additional or substitute procedural requirement would entail."[18] Properly understood, this third factor, the government's interest, should take account of the various kinds of direct and indirect harms that bad apples inflict on the good apples whom a program is designed to serve, as well as on the public more generally. (We discussed these harms in chapters 2 and 5.) Because such harms to the government's public policy interests are likely to be less immediately obvious than the private interest of the bad apple who is facing removal, the program officials and courts responsible for striking the appropriate procedural balance must be all the more careful to take them into account in conducting the *Mathews* v. *Eldridge* due process calculus.

The procedural protections afforded to potential bad apples and bad bets need not, and probably should not, be the same. In most social policy contexts, the decision concerning bad apples is whether they should be removed from a program in which they already participate. That action properly requires a higher standard of protection than a mere finding that someone does not qualify for coverage or inclusion in the first place, as is the case with bad bets. Protection procedures should also vary across programs, depending, for example, on whether the benefit is an entitlement, as with public education; a purely discretionary benefit, as with most social services; or something in between, as with public housing, where tenants acquire certain rights of continued occupancy despite the absence of an entitlement to the housing.

Tradeoffs in procedural design are inevitable. Administrative law scholar Jerry Mashaw has pointed to a number of coherent conceptions or models of administrative justice, each of which emphasizes a distinct, attractive cluster of social and legal values. Mashaw shows that "the models, while not mutually exclusive, are highly competitive: the internal logic of any one of them tends to drive the characteristics of the others from the field as it works itself out in concrete situations. . . . A compromise that works to preserve the values and to respond at once to the insights of all of these conceptions of justice will, from the perspective of each separate conception, appear incoherent and unjust."[19] Thus it may be that the best that policymakers can do is to choose the model that best fits each situation: the procedure appropriate for revoking an individual's occupational license will differ from that suitable for allocating initial benefits in a program of mass administration like Medicaid.

Here, we briefly discuss four areas of procedural protection for potential bad bets and bad apples; the optimal degree of protection will vary with the context. These areas embrace rights to the following: a statement of the reasons on which the classification was based; a hearing to rebut those reasons; an appeal of an adverse classification; and a reclassification and return to the program upon a showing that the classification was erroneous or that the conditions underlying it have materially changed.

Statement of Reasons

At a minimum, officials must inform applicants about the reasons for their adverse classifications and about the available procedures for challenging the classifications. The explanation of reasons should be sufficiently detailed to enable the bad apple or bad bet to comprehend and controvert them. A school principal need not give a written statement of reasons or allow an appeal before sending a misbehaving student home or to detention after school, but those procedures are imperative at the point where a potential classification and sanction are sufficiently damaging and severe.

Hearing

Some kind of hearing must be afforded in which the bad apple or bad bet can challenge the classification.[20] This general requirement raises a host of procedural possibilities regarding the nature of the hearing tribunal, its degree of independence from the initial decisionmaker, the adversarial or inquisitorial character of the proceeding (including possible representation by lawyers), the types and formality of evidence that may be introduced, the nature of the record on which the decision is based, the legal standard of the decision, and so forth. Each of these procedural possibilities carries potential costs and benefits that the system designers, under the *Mathews* v. *Eldridge* principle, must consider and balance.

Figure 6-5. *Appeals in Target Efficiency Screening*

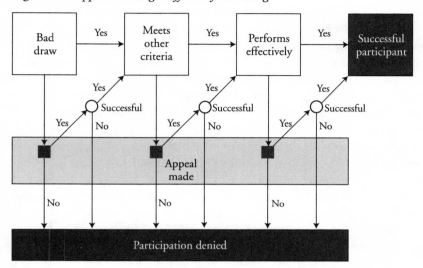

Experience in such settings as public schools, homeless shelters, and public housing, discussed in chapter 5, suggests that some past procedures may have unduly hobbled administrators in identifying and excluding bad apples before they can inflict too much harm on other participants. In such situations, expulsion delayed may be justice denied to the good apples in the program. In the case of bad bets, such as patients seeking scarce treatments for which time is of the essence, any hearing must be swift and informal; perhaps a threshold requirement could be set whereby the patient's doctor would be willing to challenge the decision on medical grounds and raise the issue with a hospital committee convened for the purpose.

Appeals

An appeals process must be a basic component of any system that seeks to accurately sort out bad apples and bad bets. The availability of an appeal can improve the accuracy of initial decisions and correct erroneous ones, albeit at a cost. If officials making the bad apple or bad bet classifications fear a reversal on appeal, they will take greater care to be accurate in the first place, for reasons of pride, reputation, career, or other concerns.

Figure 6-5 shows that the combination of criteria-based sorting and an appropriate appeals process can enable program officials to reach curve CC in figure 6-3, which produces fewer Type I and Type II errors than even BB in figure 6-2. Because CC involves only a small percentage of the applicants, it is much less expensive to administer than the individualized information-seeking process that leads to curve BB.

Decision theory also explains why an objective criteria approach with appeals, albeit imperfect, will generate much lower error costs than might be expected for the number of errors observed. The reason is that errors differ in seriousness. The individuals who are most egregiously misclassified are most likely to know this and to know that an appeal will be relatively cheap and probably successful; thus they appeal. If the agency is permitted to appeal—an important system variable—its appeals will tend to focus on Type II errors, those that wrongly included someone in a program. Here, we merely note the happy synergy between such protections and more accurate prediction for a given resource expenditure.

A right of appeal recognizes that applicants often possess information about their cases that standard administrative procedures are unlikely to uncover. Our disruptive student, for example, might know that he has two previous disruption charges but that in each case he was deemed a follower rather than a leader and that the true ringleaders have since left the school. If he believes that these factors will support his reclassification as a reasonably good apple, he is more likely to appeal the decision to send him to an alternative school. Presumably, such appeals will not be common, particularly if the appeals are not costless to the applicant. The student with four previous infractions, having little hope, is not likely to appeal, nor is the student who was fully responsible for her two previous infractions. The same is true, *mutatis mutandis,* of erroneously classified bad bets.

As with the hearing, the appeals process can be made more or less formal, taking into account the advantages and disadvantages associated with formality, including costs to the parties. Again, *Mathews* v. *Eldridge* presupposes such a calculation. For the appeals process to work, it must screen out most frivolous challenges, which means that there must be some cost to the appeal. The cost could be merely time and hassle; for low-income applicants, this would likely be the case. The program might also compensate in some fashion those individuals who do appeal and who succeed in showing that they are good apples or good bets.

Figure 6-5 expands figure 6-1 to show the mechanics of the appeals process. At each step, an individual who gets a no (that is, he is denied benefits) can appeal, and if that appeal is successful, he returns to the screening process. If unsuccessful, he is excluded from the program.

Reclassification and Return

Quite apart from an appeals process, programs must—for humane reasons and perhaps also as a matter of law—provide for the possibility that those correctly classified as bad apples will later become good ones. To provide for that happy eventuality, programs should provide a crosswalk to enable bad apples to rejoin the good apples once they have acquired the necessary tools of self-control. By easing the stigma and other negative consequences of earlier misconduct, however, crosswalks create mixed signals and incentives: they reduce the penalties for bad conduct by bad apples but also encourage their•subsequent reformation. Such crosswalks for bad apples are very common in American life, a tribute to the power of the rehabilitative ideal.[21] (The fact that three-strikes laws have produced second thoughts in California and some other states illustrates this ideal's hold on the popular imagination. Many people have come to harbor doubts about these laws because they fail to consider the severity of the crimes and they leave no scope for rehabilitation.) To the extent that policymakers have justified confidence in the remedial program to which the bad apple was sent, providing a crosswalk back to the regular one will make it easier to justify removing bad apples in the first instance.

The rehabilitation crosswalk is less applicable to bad bets. Their inability to make cost-effective use of social resources is often based on inexorable conditions, such as aging or chronic illness. However, self-improvement can turn some types of bad bets—alcoholics, for example—into better bets over time. A crosswalk for them will also be desirable. Similarly, programs should build in the flexibility to reclassify bad bets as good ones if for other reasons their situations change in ways that warrant reclassification. A patient who does not at first qualify for a kidney transplant might do so later when his condition changes.

A Way Forward

Correctly identifying bad bets and bad apples is a vital and complex challenge. We have no neat solutions to offer, and we doubt that anyone else does either. However, we believe that the framework underlying figure 6-5 offers a way forward. We wish to reach optimal point C* in figure 6-3. As a first step, to determine curve CC, we must look at the various costs of sorting more or less finely at the first stage, given that a complementary appeals process will be in place. The selection of C* itself will depend on the costs of errors of inclusion and exclusion.

If policymakers are to proceed in this direction, certain imperatives are clear. They must think more systematically about the two categories, bad bets and bad apples. They must gather the information and build the institutions that are necessary to fairly and accurately screen individuals, while establishing appropriate safeguards against errors and unfairness. With these safeguards in place, policymakers can proceed to make sound decisions about resource allocation. Accomplishing this will require technical diagnostics, classification methodologies, and hands-on program experience. It will also require close attention to the normative debates among ordinary citizens—debates about which behaviors and bets are good, bad, and in-between, and about which tradeoffs society deems acceptable. The importance of this normative debate about resource allocations in public programs, and the responsibility of officials to facilitate and structure the debate, can scarcely be exaggerated.[22] Taken together with these other measures, such efforts should yield better policies, better programs, and enhanced target efficiency.

7

Better Information, Better Targeting, and Better Policies

T he previous chapters have pointed the way toward better targeting in social programs. In this final chapter, we discuss the
steps that policymakers should take to implement our approach.
First, they must secure better information about individuals and
programs. Second, they must consider what will be done with
those who are screened out of or removed from social programs
under this better-targeting approach. Finally, once these decisions
have been made, they must apply our criteria to specific cases.

Better Information

The first step toward improving target efficiency is to generate better information about the bad bets and bad apples problems. Earlier chapters have synthesized much secondary material, showing
that in many social programs resources are going to individuals
who derive little payoff relative to other, better bets, or are going to
bad apples whose behavior diminishes the payoffs of good apple
participants. But to mobilize the necessary political support for
reform, the bad bets and bad apples problems must be carefully
assessed across a variety of programs.

For each program assessment, better information is required for
two tasks: determining which individuals should be classified as bad

bets or bad apples and assessing the extent of the bad bets and bad apples problems in each program. Although costly to obtain, such information would enable policymakers to prioritize their reform efforts and save significant resources in the long run.

Analyses of this nature can focus on categories of individuals or categories of services received—for example, a Medicare diagnosis-related group (DRG). Often, however, it will be better to assess an entire program at one time (such as a job training project), particularly if it delivers only one or a few services. In many cases, such assessments may determine that a program is worthwhile on average. Nonetheless, they are also likely to reveal considerable variability. That is, some recipients will be better bets, some worse; some will be worse apples, others better.

The incidence of bad bets and bad apples varies among programs. Bad bets pose a larger problem in some programs, such as Medicare, in which many combinations of individuals and services are not cost-effective, than they do in other programs, such as youth recreation, which tend to deliver roughly equivalent benefits at roughly equal cost to most participants. In some programs, bad bets may be rare because people who would be bad bets tend to exclude themselves. For example, people who are not manic-depressive do not want to take the costly and often unpleasant or risky medication prescribed for that condition, even if it is free. Similarly, few unqualified or uncommitted candidates are likely to apply to training programs for highly demanding and generally unappealing jobs. Job training programs, more broadly, are also likely to include fewer bad apples because trainees have no right to participate, and thus they can easily be excluded for misconduct. In contrast, we saw that bad apples plague many inner-city public schools and public housing projects.

As we saw in chapters 4 and 5, target efficiency is a greater concern when many bad apples or bad bets seek to be included in social programs. When they do, measures to screen them out or to remove them after the fact will be essential. When benefits are in the eye of the beholder, screening is an even greater challenge.[1]

Future research, then, should first identify programs that now face high net costs because of the presence of bad bets or bad apples. In some cases, these costs may be dramatically out of proportion to the numbers of individuals involved. We suspect that inner-city schools afflicted with a low percentage of chronically disruptive students are such a case. But we could not obtain solid data on the frequency, magnitude, or cost of this problem in either New York City or New Haven, where the officials in a position to know declined to help us, for various reasons.

Without concrete numbers, politicians and bureaucrats are unlikely to take action because, as we explained in chapter 3, it is usually easy for opponents of reform to make plausible countervailing arguments, such as the claim that sorting is unfair because of the risk of sorting incorrectly. But if research showed that the removal of, say, 2 percent of the students in regular classes would reduce behavior problems by, say, 80 percent, this finding might be powerful enough to cause policymakers to take notice of the bad apples problem and to seek a remedy.[2] Such research would be even more valuable if it showed that the disrupters would do just as well or better in alternative environments. Similarly, if studies showed that bad apple students could be disciplined through less onerous legal and administrative procedures that still comport with due process, this would be welcome and useful news.

Comparable research is needed on the bad bets problem in areas like health care spending, which currently accounts for more than one-seventh of the economy. Although these resources clearly produce great benefits, society could obtain substantially more for the same expenditure by avoiding bad bets and prioritizing the best of the good bets. It is the rare health insurance program that has explicit triage or rationing procedures. Indeed, most are willing to pay for nearly any nonexperimental intervention so long as a doctor approves the treatment and follows required administrative procedures. Such an approach inevitably welcomes bad bets and thus wastes program resources.[3]

A sound bad bets analysis should focus on common services rather than unusual ones. An expensive, low-benefit medical procedure that is performed only three times a year is hardly worth worrying about because the resources involved are a trivial share of our medical care budget. Indeed, the potential resources saved might be dwarfed by the administrative costs of saving them. But if at moderate cost we can identify most of the bad bets for a widely used procedure (for example, cesarean section deliveries), the savings from even a 10 percent reduction could be enormous.[4] Indeed, some programs may even prove to be *categorical* bad bets. The mortgage interest deduction for second homes may be such an example: it basically puts resources into the wrong hands (the relatively wealthy) and accomplishes no important public purpose. The principles for identifying programs where better targeting could yield greater dividends are clear. The underlying facts often are not. Future research must fill this knowledge gap.

Better Targeting

We illustrate the actual pursuit of target efficiency by returning to figure 2-1, which graphically displayed various combinations of interventions and people

Figure 7-1. *Inclusions and Exclusions Depending on Bet and Apple Status*

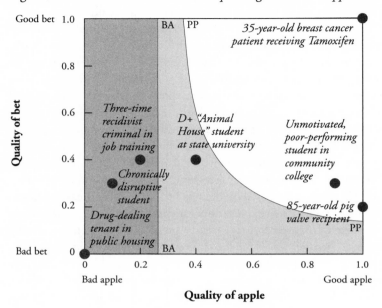

and rated them as good or bad apples and as good or bad bets. In figure 7-1, we have added two lines to the graph. The vertical line is labeled BA-BA for bad apples. The other, a curved line, is labeled PP-PP for policy preference.

Individuals in the shaded area to the left of line BA-BA are such bad apples that society does not want them in a program, regardless of how good a bet they may be. Chapter 5 explained how officials can and should make such judgments about bad apples: they should be excluded if the net benefits from their participation—what they gain minus what others lose—is negative. And because they are bad apples, society may properly give a dollar gain in their welfare less weight than a dollar loss in the welfare of good apples.

The PP-PP curve takes account of the quality of an individual-treatment pair as a bet and as an apple. It divides the policies into two parts: those accepted are above and to the right of PP-PP, and those rejected lie below and to the left of PP-PP. Thus the following individuals—who do not harm others in the program—would be deemed worthy of service: the 35-year-old breast cancer patient, the ex-smoker with lung cancer, the student doing poorly in community college, and the 85-year-old recipient of a pig valve implant. (The 85-year-old just makes it; the 90-year-old recipient discussed in chapter 5 is a worse bet and barely falls short.) The "Animal House" student—who is a bad apple because he lures other students into bad behavior and who falls into the shaded area to the right of line BA-BA—would not qualify.

The cutoff frontier is curved to show that once an individual is not so egregiously a bad apple as to be rejected out of hand, society is willing to serve individuals whose bad bet status is balanced by the fact that they are better apples and vice versa, but the rate at which it is willing to trade off these qualities varies depending on how bad a bet or apple an individual is. To see this, consider three individuals whose combination of bad bet and bad apple status places them along the frontier. Now imagine that some exogenous change—perhaps something as simple as the passage of time for a candidate for a heart valve replacement—lowers each individual's position on the good bet–bad bet scale by the same amount. A surefire good bet and relatively bad apple can easily requalify for benefits by becoming a slightly better apple. A moderately good bet and moderately good apple will have to become a much better apple to return to the cutoff frontier. And a truly bad bet and good apple may have no hope of regaining eligibility, no matter how much effort she expends in enhancing her good apple status.

Another possibly relevant policy consideration is not included in the figure, for two reasons: to keep the analysis simple and because we are agnostic about the merits of this consideration. Our analysis and graphical presentations have followed the usual, normatively attractive assumption that people should be judged as *individuals*, not as members of some larger *category*. Sometimes, however, society (or particular members) believes that devoting resources to a certain category of people implicates an important moral principle. Consider our example, discussed in chapter 2, of treating the costly category of conjoined twins. The principle in that example is that society has a moral responsibility to spend whatever medical resources are required when it can dramatically improve the quality of life. In fact, however, society's willingness to apply that principle (as distinguished from merely believing in it) may depend on the number of people in the category (here, the category of conjoined twins). Denying resources to the twins would threaten this principle whether 1 or 100 sets of twins were denied.[5] (The same is true of other principles possibly threatened by even a single violation—for example, a principle that every high school graduate, however unpromising, deserves a chance to gain a college education.) This point could be stated as rapidly diminishing marginal cost from violations of such a principle. In other words, society's discomfort about excluding a category of individuals in a program may be much less than proportional to the number of individuals so excluded.

For these reasons, the priority rating for a category—the decision as to whether its members should receive a treatment—may depend not just on the attributes of people within a category but on their numbers. Thus policymakers might decide to treat everybody in a small category A rather than treat the same number of individuals in a larger category B, even though those in B are better bets *individually* than those in A. Deciding whether the size of a category should affect its ranking will inevitably be controversial. Allowing size to matter in this way will violate the principle of assessing potential beneficiaries as individuals, while ruling size out as a factor will result in allocation decisions contrary to the preferences of individuals in society, or of some collective expression of such preferences. (This size-of-category issue is less relevant in the bad apples context where direct resource costs are less important than are other harms to the program and where one disrupter may impose almost the same costs on good apples as more disrupters in the program would.)

The curve PP-PP is contingent, not immutable. As society grows richer and as more resources become available for social programs, the cutoff curve is pushed down and to the left into the diagonal-lined area. In that event, more categories of individuals will be covered. For example, a small expansion will bring in the alcoholic liver transplant candidate. (Livers can grow again quickly, so it is feasible to use live donors, a recipient's brother, for example, instead of a cadaveric donor. Thus the reasons why scarce organs limit kidney transplants become irrelevant.) Note, however, that the PP-PP curve will never get pushed to the left of BA-BA; that is where an individual's bad apple status makes him always undesirable.

How should a program treat the bad apples or bad bets who are screened out, and which criteria and procedures should be employed in the screening process? Sometimes the answer to the first question, which we discussed in chapters 2 and 5, helps to answer the second. For example, if patients with terminal conditions were given generous and humane palliative care, then denying them costly medical treatments that will yield few quality-adjusted life years (QALYs) would be much more acceptable. If students who fail to qualify for junior college are given good options for vocational education, many marginal students may choose those options at the outset. Placing chronically disruptive students in alternative programs that give them closer supervision and a greater chance to succeed—even if those programs are somewhat more expensive to society—may soften the sting and stigma of their removal.[6]

Critics may object to the technocratic nature of our analysis. Can we really represent combinations of people and policies as points on a graph? Where do ethics and justice enter into the analysis? These are fair questions. Fortunately, they have fair answers. Although people are not points on a graph, the analyst's task is to make comparisons that foster clear thinking and to help officials who design and manage programs assess the consequences of including or excluding individuals. As we explained in chapter 3, the welfare of millions of people who received bad draws in life is at stake. Thus, merely muddling through—an all-too-common approach among program officials—is unacceptable. As the figure shows, tradeoffs are inescapable in the design of social programs. When resources are limited, some people must be excluded, and their exclusion should be the result of purposeful, well-informed decisions. Adherence to this principle, we think, promotes social justice.

Ethical analysis, moreover, supports our approach. The fact that social policy resources are limited makes it all the more important to ensure that they produce the greatest social benefit—a principle that rests on a profoundly ethical judgment. If B would derive more benefits from those resources than would A, then B should not be denied them so that they can go to A. This is a matter of fundamental fairness.

Critics may also claim that we deal with the easy cases, for which benefits and costs are easy to calculate. Although we have drawn illustrations from the social policy literature and have focused on situations for which we could find data, our methods are transparent, and we invite others to extend our approach to all manner of social programs, including those whose consequences are highly uncertain and unfold only in the long term. Such tallies, we predict, will yield optimistic findings and pessimistic ones. We have little doubt, however, that using target efficiency to guide the design of programs will lead to better returns on society's social investments.

Toward Better Policies

The journey toward improved targeting will be long, difficult, and in all likelihood only partially successful. First, when a policy area is in an amorphous state and when the key facts and values are subject to debate, the inertial force of the status quo will often be decisive. Our critics will say that we have not convinced them that this or that policy should be changed. Second, merely understanding the targeting problem, a goal that we hope this book has advanced, is not sufficient to achieve the necessary reforms. Social policy is like tennis in this respect. Knowing intellectually that you take your eye off the ball or that you fail to get into position does not ensure that you will improve your game. There are natural tendencies that distract your eye or put you in the wrong place. Careful attention, concerted effort, and practice are required to improve social policy, no less than tennis. Third, powerful forces promote bad policies in general and poorly targeted policies in particular. Chapter 3 presented many examples of these bad policies, as well as the pathologies that tend to produce them. Sometimes the causal forces are interest groups that benefit from the bad policies. In other cases, inadequate knowledge and sloppy thinking are the culprits. The interests impeding reform must be identified and counteracted, and ignorance and poor reasoning must be remedied. We hope that others will build on the analytical platform that we have constructed here.

We end with words of caution and urgency. We have noted at several points that concerns about ethics and due process must be weighed against any gains in efficiency and equity that better targeting may yield and that these concerns will sometimes trump those gains. We are proud that America is the land of the second (and often the third) chance for those who stumble. Both justice and compassion require that society try to remedy the misfortunes of bad draws, even when the bad draws bear some responsibility for their condition. Fairness demands a high degree of accuracy before classifying an individual as a bad bet or a bad apple, which is why we emphasized the importance of sound classification and appeals processes in chapter 6. Fairness also demands that society help bad bets to ease their disabilities and bad apples to redeem themselves so that they can return to the mainstream. But bending over backwards to be helpful does not mean collapsing.

Better targeting has a valuable role to play in improving social policy, despite some important values that weigh against it. Society sometimes reaches a point at which—for the sake of compassion, justice, and fairness for other bad draws—it must say: "We agree that the state is obliged to treat bad draws fairly before it classifies some of them as bad bets or bad apples. But if the costs of poor targeting are high enough, and if adequate classification and appeals procedures are in place, then we will make the hard decisions necessary to avoid bad bets and remove bad apples." The pivotal question for every social program aimed at helping bad draws is when that point has been reached. Although this question has no categorical answer, it is high time to address it candidly, creatively, systematically, and energetically. Policymakers who do so will be good bets to improve social programs and the welfare of their well-targeted participants.

Notes

Chapter 1

1. Much of our approach to thinking about resource allocations for social welfare also applies to universal entitlement programs.

2. The "undeserving poor," a term decidedly out of favor today, included not only those in social programs whose behavior harmed other participants (our bad apples) but also those who engaged in moral hazard—for example, failing to work when able to do so—to gain eligibility (who may be both bad apples and bad bets), as well as those whose behavior was self-destructive rather than harmful to others. See, generally, Michael B. Katz, *The Undeserving Poor: From the War on Poverty to the War on Welfare* (New York: Pantheon Books, 1989); Gertrude Himmelfarb, *The Idea of Poverty: England and the Early Industrial Age* (New York: Random House, 1984).

3. Examples of high-status bad apples are well-off tax cheats who increase the burdens on honest taxpayers, corporate chieftains who fleece their unsuspecting shareholders or employees while moving their assets into costly mansions in states that allow them to put primary residences beyond the reach of bankruptcy laws, prosperous couples who transfer their assets in transactions designed to qualify them for nursing-home benefits under Medicaid, and middle-class students who claim a spurious financial independence from their parents so that they can qualify for financial aid intended for the poor. These bad apples are people with the financial motivation and access to legal advice to exploit laws that are poorly targeted, carelessly drafted, or weakly enforced.

4. For evidence that the electorate is far more centrist than the politicians, see Morris P. Fiorina with Samuel J. Abrams and Jeremy C. Pope, *Culture War? The Myth of a Polarized America* (New York: Pearson Longman, 2005).

Chapter 2

1. Many of these programs score low on target efficiency in another particularly perverse sense: they benefit many good draws—people who do not suffer from misfortune and thus would not ordinarily qualify for public solicitude or governmental assistance. Examples include many recipients of Medicare, heavily subsidized tuition at public universities, and student loans issued at below-market rates. The major argument for including good draws is to increase political support for various programs by spreading the benefits more widely. For example, the universality of Social Security retirement benefits, along with its contributory feature, importantly promotes the program's popularity. We touch on this issue in chapters 6 and 7.

2. See chapter 4 for more discussion of this issue.

3. Public and private colleges increasingly admit high school dropouts; see Karen W. Arenson, "Can't Complete High School? Go Right to College," *New York Times*, May 30, 2006, p. A1.

4. In fiscal year 2005, a decade after Congress enacted a law phasing out the subsidies over seven years, the government paid a record $23 billion to farmers. According to one analysis, 72 percent of this sum went to 10 percent of the recipients, who are typically much wealthier than the average taxpayer. Little of the money went to poor farmers. Scott Kilman and Roger Thurow, "In Fight Against Farm Subsidies, Even Farmers Are Joining Foes," *Wall Street Journal*, March 14, 2006, p. A1.

5. See Edward L. Glaeser and Jesse M. Shapiro,"The Benefits of the Home Mortgage Interest Deduction," Discussion Paper 1979 (Cambridge, Mass.: Harvard Institute of Economic Research, October 2002). To be sure, the deductibility of mortgage interest is presently incorporated into the price of housing and in that sense is not a continuing subsidy. However, removing deductibility would impose a windfall loss for home owners.

6. Bad apples are also bad bets when their participation in a public program will have few social benefits, particularly if the program was intended to avoid their kind of misconduct. An example would be students who wrongfully get food stamps but who would eat well without them.

7. Daniel Patrick Moynihan, "Defining Deviancy Down," *American Scholar* (Winter 1993): 17–30.

8. See the discussion of the probability weighting functions in Daniel Kahneman and Amos Tversky, "Prospect Theory: An Analysis of Decision under Risk," *Econometrica* 47, no. 2 (1979): 280–94. It shows that individuals tend to respond little to differences in low but positive probabilities.

9. Daniel Kahneman, Paul Slovic, and Amos Tversky, eds., *Judgment under Uncertainty: Heuristics and Biases* (Cambridge University Press, 1982).

10. See Martin Gilens, *Why Americans Hate Welfare: Race, Media, and the Politics of Antipoverty Policy* (University of Chicago Press, 1999). As Gilens's study shows, public

perceptions about bad apples are sometimes wrong, and they can be wrong in many different ways. And when they are, officials have an obligation to explain why this is so. Joe Soss and Sanford F. Schram in "A Public Transformed? Welfare Reform as Policy Feedback?" *American Political Science Review* (forthcoming) argue that the symbolism associated with policies, not their actual structure or performance, is what predominantly affects mass opinion. Thus the mass media, elite opinion, and social conversation play an important role in shaping public attitudes. To the extent that this is true, explicit discussion of target efficiency, by itself, would help reshape public attitudes. Although Soss and Schram present quotes from leading experts Hugh Heclo, Christopher Jencks, Lawrence Mead, and Mickey Kaus indicating that welfare reform changed public attitudes towards greater acceptance of welfare, they put more credence in cited survey evidence that is contrary to these experts' views.

11. The extent to which illegal immigrants consume resources intended for others is a much-debated question among labor economists and immigration experts. Undocumented aliens consume many social resources, such as public schools, publicly subsidized health care, and law enforcement. On the other hand, they are taxpayers, productive workers, and often urban entrepreneurs. There is considerable disagreement over the magnitudes of these costs and benefits and even about their relevance to the proper enforcement of our immigration laws. For a discussion of studies and competing explanations of immigration, see Peter H. Schuck, *Citizens, Strangers, and In-Betweens: Essays on Immigration and Citizenship* (Boulder, Colo.: Westview, 1998), pp. 337–41.

12. On hospital costs, see Christopher J. Zook and Francis D. Moore, "High-Cost Users of Medical Care," *New England Journal of Medicine* 302 (1980): 996–1002. The authors found that hospital costs were concentrated on a few patients; on average, these high-cost patients (13 percent) consumed as many resources as did the low-cost patients (87 percent). For a recent account of resource drains, see Malcolm Gladwell, "Million-Dollar Murray," *New Yorker*, February 13 and 20, 2006, pp. 96–103. He describes people who fall into a number of these categories simultaneously and impose extremely high costs on the social services system, such as a substance abuser whose costs totaled $65,000 in only three months, 2,500 hardcore homeless individuals who were sheltered at a cost of $62 million a year, and 15 chronically homeless inebriates who were treated in hospital emergency rooms 417 times over eighteen months, running up medical bills averaging $100,000 during this period. On long-term welfare recipients, see, for example, Mary Jo Bane and David R. Ellwood, *Welfare Realities: From Rhetoric to Reform* (Harvard University Press, 1994); for government data on welfare dependency, see U.S. Department of Health and Human Services, *Indicators of Welfare Dependence: Annual Report to Congress 2004*, especially section II, indicators 7–9 (aspe.hhs.gov/hsp/indicators04/index.htm).

13. See, generally, Jerry L. Mashaw, *Due Process in the Administrative State* (Yale University Press, 1985).

14. Although this well-being is ordinarily measured by individuals' self-assessments, society tends to be more paternalistic toward groups whose rational choices are compromised by immaturity, ignorance, or lack of free will—for example, children, the uninformed, and addicts. Arguably, addicts possess some degree of free will when they make the choices that lead to their initial addictions and perhaps even their subsequent ones as

well. Individuals' beliefs about free will may affect whether they consider addicts to be bad bets, bad apples, or just bad draws.

15. See Edith Stokey and Richard Zeckhauser, *A Primer for Policy Analysis* (New York: W.W. Norton, 1978), pp. 134–58, for a detailed discussion of benefit-cost and cost-effectiveness analyses.

16. John Rawls, *A Theory of Justice* (Harvard University Press, 1971).

17. See Richard J. Zeckhauser, "Risk Spreading and Distribution," in *Redistribution through Public Choice*, edited by Harold M. Hochman and George E. Peterson (Columbia University Press, 1974), pp. 206–28.

18. Arthur C. Brooks, *Who Cares: The Surprising Truth About Who Is Charitable, Who Isn't, and Why It Matters for America* (New York: Basic Books, forthcoming). Some of this private charity supports public goods, such as cancer research, that will benefit the poor but mostly the nonpoor. The greatest redistribution to the poor, however, occurs only when politicians, on behalf of voters, bind themselves to contribute collectively through taxes.

19. A recent nationally representative Internet-based survey asked respondents to classify themselves as an above-average, average, or below-average fatality risk from natural disasters. Of those classifying themselves as average or below average, 81.8 percent favored government programs to assist victims of natural disasters. See table 6 of W. Kip Viscusi and Richard J. Zeckhauser, "National Survey Evidence on Disasters and Relief," in *Journal of Risk and Uncertainty* (forthcoming).

20. See, for example, Jacob S. Hacker, "After Welfare," *New Republic*, October 11, 2004, pp. 46–47 (reviewing Jason DeParle, *American Dream: Ten Kids and a Nation's Drive to End Welfare* [New York: Viking, 2004]). The same is true of most tax expenditures; see Christopher Howard, *The Hidden Welfare State: Tax Expenditures and Social Policy in the United States* (Princeton University Press, 1999) for data comparing transfer programs with various categories of tax expenditures.

21. In addition, factors other than cost-effectiveness often influence voters' preferences. For example, the race of the voter and of the presumed recipient powerfully predicts the support for government redistribution. See Alberto Alesina and Edward L. Glaeser, *Fighting Poverty in the US and Europe: A World of Difference* (Oxford University Press, 2004); see also Gilens, *Why Americans Hate Welfare*.

22. See Henry J. Aaron and William B. Schwartz with Melissa Cox, *Can We Say No? The Challenge of Rationing Health Care* (Brookings, 2005).

23. See, for example, Michael Chernew and others, "Managed Care and Medical Technology: Implications for Cost Growth," *Health Affairs* 16, no. 2 (1997): pp. 196–206. For discussions on specific drugs, see Alex Berenson, "Cancer Drugs Offer Hope, But at Huge Expense," *New York Times*, July 12, 2005, p. A1, and Sarah Lyall, "Court Backs Briton's Right to a Costly Drug," *New York Times*, April 13, 2006, p. A3.

24. "The Health Care Crisis and What to Do about It," *New York Review of Books*, March 23, 2006, pp. 42–43 (reviewing Henry J. Aaron and others, *Can We Say No?* and citing health economist Uwe Reinhardt).

25. See Katharine Q. Seelye and John Tierney, "E.P.A. Drops Age-Based Cost Studies," *New York Times*, May 8, 2003, p. A34.

26. See Malcolm Gladwell, "Million-Dollar Murray." This case is also discussed in chapter 5.

27. The New York City and New Haven, Connecticut, school systems repeatedly declined to share data on their alternative programs.

Chapter 3

1. Congressional Budget Office, "Table 11, Deficits, Surpluses, Debt and Related Series 1965–2005," in "Historical Budget Data," January 26, 2006 (www.cbo.gov/budget/historical.pdf).

2. Robert Pear, "Finances of Social Security and Medicare Deteriorate," *New York Times*, May 2, 2006, p. A23; Peter R. Orzag and John B. Shoven, "Social Security," in *Restoring Fiscal Sanity 2005: Meeting the Long Run Challenge*, edited by Alice M. Rivlin and Isabel Sawhill (Brookings, 2005), pp. 59–60.

3. Robert Pear, "Finances of Social Security and Medicare Deteriorate." The Congressional Budget Office estimates that federal spending for Medicare and Medicaid will increase from 4.2 percent of GDP today to 5.9 percent in ten years. Congressional Budget Office, "The Budget and Economic Outlook, Fiscal Years 2007 to 2016," January 2006, p. 52, table 3.1 (www.cbo.gov/ftpdoc.cfm?index=7027&type=1).

4. See, for example, Pam Belluck and Katie Zezima, "Massachusetts Legislation on Insurance Becomes Law," *New York Times*, April 13, 2006, p. A1. For a review of state initiatives in 2002 to expand access to health insurance without federal funds, see Neva Kaye, Mimi Marchev, and Trish Riley, *Building a Pathway to Universal Coverage: How Do We Get From Here to There?* (Portland, Maine: National Academy for State Health Policy, November 2002) (www.nashp.org/Files/GNL49_FTF_III.pdf). For a discussion of state fiscal constraints, see David A. Super, "Rethinking Fiscal Federalism," *Harvard Law Review* 118, no. 8 (2005): 2544–652.

5. For examples, see Malcolm Gladwell, "Million-Dollar Murray," *New Yorker*, February 13 and 20, 2006, pp. 96–103.

6. See David Cay Johnston, "Overstating of Assets Is Seen to Cost U.S. Billions in Taxes," *New York Times*, January 24, 2005, p. C2. This may be changing. Tom Herman, "Research Shows Fighting IRS Is Often Worth It," *Wall Street Journal*, May 17, 2006, p. D1. The IRS is auditing more returns, cracking down on high-income individuals and tax shelters, and contracting with private debt collectors.

7. See David Cay Johnston, "Overstating of Assets Is Seen to Cost U.S. Billions in Taxes."

8. See, for example, Steven Greenhouse, "Going After Migrants, but Not Employers," *New York Times*, April 16, 2006, p. WK3. Agents assigned to enforcement of worksites plunged from 240 in 1999 to 65 in 2004; notices of intent to fine employers dropped from 417 in 1999 to 3 in 2004; criminal actions increased. Eduardo Porter, "The Search for Illegal Immigrants Stops at the Workplace," *New York Times*, March 5, 2006, p. BU3. Few employers are participating in a pilot program set up to improve data matching. Government Accountability Office, *Immigration Enforcement: Weaknesses Hinder Employment Verification and Worksite Enforcement Efforts*, GAO-05-813, August 2005, pp. 35–36

(www.gao.gov/new.items/d05813.pdf). However, see Eric Lipton, "U.S. Crackdown Set Over Hiring Of Immigrants," *New York Times*, April 21, 2006, p. A1.

9. Henry J. Aaron and William B. Schwartz with Melissa Cox, *Can We Say No? The Challenge of Rationing Health Care* (Brookings, 2005), chapter 1.

10. Paul L. Burgess, "Compliance with Unemployment Insurance Job Search Regulations," *Journal of Law and Economics* 35, no. 2 (1992): 373–75.

11. In 1993 the U.S. Department of Labor reported that more than 1 million workers suffer back injuries each year and that back injuries account for 20 percent of all compensation claims costing industry billions of dollars. Department of Labor, "Back Injuries— Nation's Number One Workplace Safety Problem," Fact Sheet No. OSHA 93-09, January 1, 1993.

12. For a taxonomy of entitlements, see David A. Super, "The Political Economy of Entitlement," *Columbia Law Review* 104, no. 3 (2004): 633.

13. Ruth L. Kirschstein, *Insurance Parity for Mental Health: Cost, Access, and Quality*, final report to Congress by the National Advisory Mental Health Counsel, NIH Publication No. 00-4787 (Department of Health and Human Services, National Institutes of Health, National Institute of Mental Health, June 2000), p. 7 (www.nimh.nih.gov/publicat/nimhparity). But see Robert Pear, "Study Backs Equal Coverage for Mental Ills," *New York Times*, March 30, 2006, p. A19. See Edwin Park and others, "The Troubling Medicare Legislation," Center on Budget and Policy Priorities, revised December 8, 2003 (www.cbpp.org/11-18-03health2.htm).

14. For a discussion on moral hazard and adverse selection, see Edwin Park and others, "The Troubling Medicare Legislation"; David Cutler and Richard Zeckhauser, "The Anatomy of Health Insurance," in *The Handbook of Health Economics*, edited by Joseph P. Newhouse and Anthony J. Culyer (Amsterdam: Elsevier Science, 2000), pp. 563–643.

15. Jonathan Klick and Thomas Stratmann, "Diabetes Treatments and Moral Hazard," Public Law Research Paper 159, Florida State University College of Law.

16. See David A. Moss, *When All Else Fails: Government as the Ultimate Risk Manager* (Harvard University Press, 2002), pp. 311–25; General Accounting Office [changed in 2004 to Government Accountability Office], *Financial Management: Status of the Governmentwide Efforts to Address Improper Payment Problems*, GAO-04-09, October 2003 (www.gao.gov/new.items/d0499.pdf).

17. Joseph B. Treaster and Cornelia Dean, "Yet Another Victim of Katrina," *New York Times*, January 6, 2006, p. C1.

18. Personal communication from Jerry L. Mashaw, Sterling Professor of Law, Yale University, December 27, 2005.

19. The Personal Responsibility and Work Opportunity Reconciliation Act of 1996, Public Law 104-193, 110 Stat. 2260.

20. "Relatively good apples" because efforts are afoot to tighten the standards and move more of the remaining recipients off the rolls. Robert Pear, "New Rules Force States to Curb Welfare Rolls," *New York Times*, June 28, 2006, p. A14. See Ron Haskins, *Work over Welfare: The Inside Story of the 1996 Welfare Reform Law* (Brookings, forthcoming 2006). The Temporary Assistance for Needy Families (TANF) program gives the states

significant discretion in spending TANF funds. Many states use some of their funds for job training, child support, and other work-related programs rather than to funnel them directly to program recipients. Federal rules issued in 2006 may limit this discretion.

21. U.S. House Ways and Means Committee, "Background Materials and Data on the Programs within the Jurisdiction of the Committee on Ways and Means" (2004), tables 9-26 to 9-29, pp. 9-52–9-58 (waysandmeans.house.gov/Documents.asp?section=813).

22. See Peter H. Schuck, "Immigrants' Political and Legal Incorporation in the United States after 9/11: Two Steps Forward, One Step Back," Yale Law School, unpublished manuscript, August 11, 2006.

23. Internal Revenue Service, "Compliance Estimates for Earned Income Tax Credit Claimed on 1997 Returns," September 2000; IRS, "Compliance Estimates for Earned Income Tax Credit Claimed on 1999 Returns," February 28, 2002 (www.irs.gov/pub/irs-soi/compeitc.pdf).

24. See Office of Management and Budget, *Improving the Accuracy and Integrity of Federal Payments*, February 2, 2006, table 2, footnote 6 (http://www.whitehouse.gov/omb/financial/fia/improv_accuracy_fed_payments.pdf). See Jeffrey Liebman, "The EITC Compliance Problem," *Joint Center for Poverty Research News* 2, no. 3 (Summer 1998) (www.jcpr.org/98summer/article3.html).

25. As a result of increased enforcements efforts directed at EITC fraud, IRS audits disproportionately targeted the working poor for audits. David Cay Johnston, "I.R.S. More Likely to Audit the Poor and Not the Rich," *New York Times,* April 16, 2000. This income-based differential in audit rates remains today. See Transactional Records Access Clearinghouse, "Combined District Plus Compliance (Service) Center Audits, IRS Audit Rates by Individual Audit Class: Nonbusiness and Business Returns, FYs 1988 Through 2004," Syracuse University (trac.syr.edu/tracirs/highlights/current/ratesTab3.html [March 2006]). Personal communication from David A. Super, professor of law, University of Maryland, July 10, 2006.

26. David A. Super, "The Quiet 'Welfare' Revolution: Resurrecting the Food Stamp Program in the Wake of the 1996 Welfare Law," *New York University Law Review* 79, no. 4 (2004): 1271, 1296.

27. Ibid., p. 1381.

28. Sewell Chan, "Mayor Overrules 2 Aides Seeking Food Stamp Shift," *New York Times,* April 18, 2006, p. A1.

29. Personal communication from David A. Super, June 28, 2006, and July 10, 2006; personal communication from Stacy Dean, director, food stamp policy, Center on Budget Policy and Priorities, June 26, 2006.

30. Personal communication from Christopher Jencks, Malcolm Wiener Professor of Social Policy, John F. Kennedy School of Government, Harvard University, November 9, 2004.

31. Robert Pear, "States' Pocketbooks Are Fuller, but Health Costs Stall Recovery," *New York Times*, December 17, 2004, p. A26.

32. Douglas J. Besharov and Caeli A. Higney, "Federal and State Child Care Expenditures, 1997–2003: Rapid Growth Followed by Steady Spending," report prepared for the

Administration on Children, Youth, and Families, Administration for Children and Families, Department of Health and Human Services (2006) (www.welfareacademy.org/pubs/childcare/childcarespending.pdf). Personal communication from David A. Super, July 10, 2006.

33. Personal communication from Christopher Jencks, November 9, 2004. See also Scott Winship and Christopher Jencks, "Understanding Welfare Reform," *Harvard Magazine* 107, no. 2 (November-December 2004): 34–35.

34. Christopher Jencks, "Liberal Lessons from Welfare Reform: Why Welfare-to-Work Turned Out Better Than We Expected, and What to Do Next," *American Prospect*, July 15, 2002, p. A9.

35. For one such investigation, see Ron Haskins, *Work over Welfare.*

36. See Robert F. Schoeni and Rebecca M. Blank, "What has Welfare Reform Accomplished? Impacts on Welfare Participation, Employment, Income, Poverty, and Family Structure" (Ann Arbor: Gerald R. Ford School of Public Policy, University of Michigan, and National Bureau of Economic Research, February 2000) (www.fordschool.umich.edu/research/papers/PDFfiles/00-016.pdf). They provide a thoughtful review of PRWORA and of state reform programs on rates of poverty and welfare participation.

37. Searches were conducted using both Lexis-Nexis and ProQuest; the results were quite similar. Data on file with the authors.

38. Guido Calabresi and Philip Bobbitt, *Tragic Choices* (New York: W.W. Norton, 1978).

39. For an interesting example of such legal procedures, see James Q. Whitman, *The Origins of Reasonable Doubt: Religious Roots of the Criminal Trial* (Yale University Press, forthcoming 2007). Whitman distinguishes between "moral comfort" procedures and "proof" procedures.

40. David A. Super provides other examples of opaque processes: federalism in general, block grants in particular, conference committees, and fast track procedures for approving military base closures and trade agreements. Personal communication, July 10, 2006.

41. See, for example, Terry Moe, "The Politics of Bureaucratic Structure," in *Can the Government Govern?* edited by John E. Chubb and Paul E. Peterson (Brookings, 1989).

42. For one analysis of this evasion, see David A. Super, "The New Moralizers," *Columbia Law Review* 104 (2004): 2032–96.

43. Personal communication from Christopher Jencks, November 9, 2004.

44. See Ron Haskins, *Work over Welfare.*

45. One of us has argued for greater candor in our social discourse about ethno-racial issues. See Peter H. Schuck, *Diversity in America: Keeping Government at a Safe Distance* (Cambridge, Mass.: Belknap Press, 2006), pp. 332–33. See also Orlando Patterson, *Rituals of Blood: Consequences of Slavery in Two American Centuries* (New York: Basic Civitas, 1998), especially chapter 1.

46. Daniel Patrick Moynihan, "The Negro Family: The Case for National Action," Office of Policy Planning and Research, U.S. Department of Labor, March 1965, in Lee Rainwater and William L. Yancey, *The Moynihan Report and the Politics of Controversy* (MIT Press, 1967) .

47. On unions, see James B. Jacobs, *Mobsters, Unions, and Feds: The Mafia and the American Labor Movement* (New York University Press, 2006). On clergy abuse, see Bishop Wilton D. Gregory, presidential address to annual meeting of United States Conference of Catholic Bishops, Dallas, Texas, June 13, 2002, reprinted in *Shaken by Scandals: Catholics Speak Out about Priests' Sexual Abuse,* edited by Paul Thigpen (Ann Arbor, Mich.: Servant Publications, 2002), p. 222.

48. This group of bad policies, of course, is very large. Tax enforcement, as discussed in this chapter, is but one example.

49. An example is the monopoly of the United States Postal Service over first-class mail.

50. For a discussion and list of such programs, see Chris Edwards, "Downsizing the Federal Government," *Policy Analysis* 515 (June 2004) (www.cato.org/pubs/pas/pa515.pdf [March 2006]).

51. Examples include state-enforced cartels in urban transportation, bank charters, and certain occupations.

52. For the theory, see, for example, Glenn Blackmon and Richard J. Zeckhauser, "Fragile Commitments and the Regulatory Process," *Yale Journal of Regulation* 9, no. 1 (Winter 1992): 73. For a recent example, see Michael Janofsky, "Judges Overturn Bush Bid to Ease Pollution Rules," *New York Times,* March 18, 2006, p. A1. The ruling leaves industry uncertain about future pollution control investments.

53. Sometimes the official discretion may be so great as to be unconstitutional. See, for example, *Papachristou* v. *City of Jacksonville,* 405 U.S. 156 (1972), which invalidated an antiloitering ordinance for this reason, among others.

54. The federal sentencing guidelines, which unduly constrain judges' discretion, are an example. Kate Stith and Jose A. Cabranes, *Fear of Judging: Sentencing Guidelines in the Federal Courts* (University of Chicago Press, 1998). Another is the 1996 immigration statute, which bars officials from making exceptions to mandates of detention and removal. Peter H. Schuck, *Citizens, Strangers, and In-Betweens: Essays on Immigration and Citizenship* (Boulder, Colo.: Westview, 1998), p. 145.

55. For some unconventional examples, see David A. Bernstein, *You Can't Say That! The Growing Threat to Civil Liberties from Antidiscrimination Laws* (Washington: Cato Institute, 2003).

56. On moral hazard for private actors, see this chapter. On moral hazard for government actors, illegal immigrants provide an interesting example. The federal government receives most of the tax revenue from the labor of undocumented immigrants while bearing few of the costs they create, which fall primarily on local governments. Peter H. Schuck, *Citizens, Strangers, and In-Betweens,* chapter 8.

57. Charles T. Clotfelter and others, "State Lotteries at the Turn of the Century: A Report to the National Gambling Impact Study Commission," June 1999.

58. A classic example is the "bridge to nowhere" included in pork barrel legislation enacted in 2005 at the behest of Senator Ted Stevens of Alaska. See *Washington Post,* "Mr. Stevens's Tirade," October 23, 2005, p. B6.

59. See, for example, James Baron, "Many Saw Free Air-Conditioner In Post-9/11 Clean-Air Program," *New York Times,* Nov. 2, 2004, p. A1. About 62 percent of those

reimbursed for air quality products, roughly 140,000 people, were not eligible. See also Eric Lipton, " 'Breathtaking' Waste and Fraud in Hurricane Aid," *New York Times*, June 27, 2006, p. A1.

60. Although regressive redistribution violates norms of fairness (and sometimes efficiency) that are widely embraced by American society, there are many examples of such policies: mortgage deductions, farm subsidies, subsidized student loans and low in-state college tuition, untaxed Social Security benefits, tax deductions rather than credits, and stepped-up tax basis for securities held at death, to name just a few. Americans do tolerate significantly greater inequalities than do the citizens of other developed democracies, who support more state-sponsored redistribution. Alberto Alesina and Edward L. Glaeser, *Fighting Poverty in the US and Europe: A World of Difference* (Oxford University Press, 2004).

61. A well-known study published in the early 1990s found no impact of an increased minimum wage on employment in fast food restaurants. David Card and Alan Krueger, "Minimum Wage and Employment: A Case Study of the Fast-Food Industry in New Jersey and Pennsylvania," *American Economic Review* 84, no. 4 (1994): 772–93. However, a survey in the Winter 2005 issue of the *Journal of Economic Perspectives* indicates that two-thirds of academic economists at top universities agree with the statement "a minimum wage increases unemployment among young and unskilled." See also Scott J. Adams and David Neumark, "The Effects of Living Wage Laws: Evidence from Failed and Derailed Living Wage Campaigns," Working Paper No. 2004-11 (San Francisco: Public Policy Institute of California, August 2004). They found that these campaigns increased wages of low-wage workers but also reduced employment among the least skilled.

62. Charles Monroe Haar, *Between the Idea and the Reality: A Study in the Origin, Fate, and Legacy of the Model Cities Program* (Boston: Little, Brown, 1975), pp. 217–18.

63. Dean E. Murphy, "Security Grants Still Streaming to Rural States," *New York Times*, October 12, 2004, p. A1. Diane Cardwell and Al Baker, "For the Most Part, That's A Secret," *New York Times*, June 3, 2006, p. A1.

64. For a fuller development of these points, see Martha B. Coven, "The Freedom to Spend: The Case for Cash Based Public Assistance," *Minnesota Law Review* 86 (2002): 847.

65. For three examples, see Charles A. Reich, "The New Property," *Yale Law Journal* 73 (1964): 773; Mary Ann Glendon, *Rights Talk: The Impoverishment of Political Discourse* (New York: Free Press, 1991); and Robert A. Kagan, *Adversarial Legalism: The American Way of Law* (Harvard University Press, 2001).

66. Sometimes the courts oblige them. For some examples, see Peter H. Schuck, *Meditations of A Militant Moderate: Cool Views on Hot Topics* (Lanham, Md.: Rowman & Littlefield, 2006), pp. 103–14.

67. See Eugene Volokh, "The Mechanisms of the Slippery Slope," *Harvard Law Review* 116 (2003): 1026.

68. Thomas C. Schelling, *Choice and Consequence: Perspectives of an Errant Economist* (Harvard University Press, 1985).

69. Herbert A. Simon, *Administrative Behavior* (New York: Free Press, 1947); Charles E. Lindblom, "The Science of Muddling Through," *Public Administration Review* 19 (1959): 79–88.

Chapter 4

Sources for Table 4-1. The information in this table and accompanying citations is taken from similar tables produced by the Cost Effectiveness Analysis Registry, maintained by the Tufts-New England Medical Center, Comprehensive Table of Cost-Utility Ratios 2002–2003 and Comprehensive Table of Cost-Utility 1976–2001 (www.tufts-nemc.org/cearegistry [accessed March 2006]).

[A] Rianne Oostenbrink and colleagues, "Cost-Utility Analysis of Patient Care in Children with Meningeal Signs," *International Journal of Technology Assessment in Health Care,* 18, no. 3 (2002): 485–96.

[B] M.R. Arguedas and colleagues, "The Cost-Effectiveness of Hepatitis A Vaccination in Patients with Chronic Hepatitis C Viral Infection in the United States," *Am J. Gastroenterology,* 97 (2002): 731.

[C] K. Stein and colleagues, Screening for Hepatitis C in Genito-Urinary Medicine Clinics: A Cost Utility Analysis, *J. Hepatology,* 814 (2003).

[D] B.R. Jackson and colleagues, "The Cost-Effectiveness of NAT for HIV, HCV, and HBV in Whole-Blood Donations, *Transfusion,* 43, no. 6 (2003): 721–9.

[E–G] D. Hershman and colleagues, "Outcomes of Tamoxifen Chemoprevention for Breast Cancer in Very High-Risk Women: A Cost-Effectiveness Analysis," *Journal of Clinical Oncology,* 20 (2002): 9.

[H–J] P.J. Mahadevia and colleagues, "Lung Cancer Screening with Helical Computed Tomography in Older Adult Smokers: A Decision and Cost-Effectiveness Analysis," *JAMA,* 289 (2003): 313.

[K] S.J. Lee and colleagues, "The Costs and Cost-Effectiveness of Unrelated Donor Bone Marrow Transplantation for Chronic Phase Myelogenous Leukemia," *Blood,* 92 (1998): 4047.

[L] M.B. Hamel and colleagues, "Cost-Effectiveness of Aggressive Care for Patients with Nontraumatic Coma," *Critical Care Medicine,* 30 (2002): 1191.

[M–O] R.B. Forbes and colleagues, "Population Based Cost Utility Study of Interferon Beta-1b in Secondary Progressive Multiple Sclerosis," *British Medical Journal,* 319 (1999): 1529.

[P] D. Polsky and colleagues, "Economic Evaluation of Breast Cancer Treatment: Considering the Value of Patient Choice," *Journal of Clinical Oncology,* 21 (2003): 1139.

[Q] S. Goodacre, "Cost Effectiveness Analysis of Diagnostic Strategies for Patients with Acute, Undifferentiated Chest Pain," *Emergency Medical Journal,* 20 (2003): 429.

[R] W.F. Fearon and colleagues, "Cost-Effectiveness of Measuring Fractional Flow Reserve to Guide Coronary Interventions," *American Heart Journal,* 145 (2003): 882.

[S] H.M. Nathoe and colleagues, "A Comparison of On Pump and Off Pump Coronary Bypass Surgery in Low-Risk Patients," *New England Journal of Medicine,* 348 (2003): 394.

[T] V. Vella, "Potential Costs and Effects of the National Service Framework for Coronary Heart Disease in the UK," *Pharmaeconomics,* 21 (2003): 49.

[U] D. Yin, "Cost-Effectiveness of Screening for Asymptomatic Carotid Stenosis," *Journal of Vascular Surgery,* 27 (1998):245.

[V] K.H. Lee and colleagues,"Cardiopulmonary Resuscitation: What Cost to Cheat Death?" *Critical Care Medicine*, 24 (1996): 2046.

[W] H.B. Highland and colleagues,"Treatment of Pulmonary Arterial Hypertension: A Preliminary Decision Analysis," *Chest*, 124, no. 6 (2003): 2087.

[X] S.D. Ramsey and colleagues, "The Cost-Effectiveness of Lung Transplantation. A Pilot Study," University of Washington Medical Center Lung Transplant Study Group [comment], *Chest*, 108 (1995): 1594–601.

[Y–AA] S.V. Jassal, "Kidney Transplantation in the Elderly: A Decision Analysis," *Journal Soc. Nephrol*, 14, no. 1 (2003): 187–96.

[AB] W. Hollingworth and colleagues,"Rapid Magnetic Resonance Imaging For Diagnosing Cancer-Related Back Pain," *Journal of General Internal Medicine*, 18, no. 4 (2003): 303–12.

[AC] L.S. Medina and colleagues,"Children with Suspected Craniosynostosis: A Cost-Effectiveness Analysis of Diagnostic Strategies," *AJR Am J Roentgenol*, 179, no. 1 (2002): 215–21.

[AD] M.B. Hamel and colleagues,"Outcomes and Cost-Effectiveness of Initiating Dialysis and Continuing Aggressive Care in Seriously Ill Hospitalized Adults," *Annals of Internal Medicine*, 127 (1997): 195–202.

1. David Blumenthal and Richard Zeckhauser, "The Artificial Heart as an Economic Issue," in *After Barney Clark: Reflections on the Utah Artificial Heart Program*, edited by Margery W. Shaw (University of Texas Press, 1984), pp. 149–67. It is still not part of our medical armamentarium, despite modest past successes, because many recipients would be bad bets.

2. See Ron Haskins and Isabel V. Sawhill, "Work and Marriage: The Way to End Poverty and Welfare," Policy Brief: Welfare Reform and Beyond no. 28 (Brookings, September 2003). The simulation indicates that if every family head had a high school education and earned what high school graduates earned, the poverty rate among families with children would decline by nearly two percentage points.

3. For an example of using such courses in college admissions, see Peter H. Schuck, *Diversity in America: Keeping Government at a Safe Distance* (Harvard University Press, 2003), p. 184.

4. Guido Calabresi and Philip Bobbitt, *Tragic Choices* (New York: W. W. Norton, 1978).

5. Donald Shepard and Richard Zeckhauser,"Where Now for Saving Lives?" *Law and Contemporary Problems* 40, no. 4 (1976): 5–45. See also Matthew D. Adler, "QALYs and Policy Evaluation: A New Perspective," *Yale Journal of Health Policy, Law, and Ethics* 6, no. 1 (2006): 1.

6. This scaling would imply that a person who has two years to live but who will be in severe pain would accept an operation with 50 percent mortality if it would eliminate the pain. Either way, the patient would secure one QALY on average. Discounting of QALYs, ordinarily employed, is not a key consideration for a one- or two-year life span.

7. See generally Orley C. Ashenfelter, "Measuring the Value of a Statistical Life: Problems and Prospects," IZA Discussion Paper 1911 (Bonn: Institute for the Study of Labor, January 2006).

8. W. Kip Viscusi and Joseph E. Aldy, "The Value of a Statistical Life: A Critical Review of Market Estimates throughout the World," *Journal of Risk and Uncertainty* 27, no. 1 (2003): 5. These same authors compute the value of a life year at various ages, finding a value of $263,000 at age 30. W. Kip Viscusi and Joseph E. Aldy, "Age Variations in Workers' Value of Statistical Life," Harvard Olin Discussion Paper 468 (Cambridge, Mass: National Bureau of Economic Research, 2004).

9. More explicitly, the logarithm of the required expenditures has the traditional, bell-shaped, normal distribution. Medical expenses across citizens in a year have roughly a log-normal distribution, and dollars to QALY expenditures are likely to approximate such a distribution.

10. These data were taken from the Tufts–New England Medical School's Cost Effectiveness Registry, which lists nearly all such studies conducted (apparently worldwide) since the late 1970s.

11. Gardiner Harris, "Panel Unanimously Recommends Cervical Cancer Vaccine for Girls 11 and Up," *New York Times*, June 30, 2006, p. A10.

12. Allen R. Myerson, "Ideas and Trends; Final Stats: Mantle's Law Medical Bills," *New York Times*, August 20, 1995, sec.4, p. A5.

13. Ibid.

14. One prominent surgeon refers to the allure of "those pesky little miracles," personal communication from Dr. Randolph Reinhold, chairman of surgery, Hospital of Saint Raphael, New Haven, Conn., July 11, 2005.

15. American Medical Association, Code of Ethics, §2.03 Allocation of Limited Medical Resources. Appendix One, *infra*, contains all excerpts from the code of ethics related to futile care determinations.

16. The Supreme Court of Canada has held that the government's health agency may not bar individuals from purchasing private health care in situations when receiving care in the public system would take too long. *Chaoulli* v. *Quebec*, 1 S.C.R. 791 (2005) (scc.lexum.umontreal.ca/en/2005/2005scc35/2005scc35.html). The European Court of Justice has ruled that the British government must pay the costs of patients who seek treatment elsewhere in the European Union because of undue delay in getting treatment at home. Sarah Lyall, "Britain: Delayed Patients Can Have Operations Abroad," *New York Times*, May 17, 2006, p. A8.

17. See, for example, Stephen Breyer, *Breaking the Vicious Circle* (Harvard University Press, 1993). Breyer reports a government study of a variety of regulations intended to save lives. The costs (in 1990 dollars) for a premature death avoided ranged from $100,000 (ban on unvented space heaters) to $92 billion (atrazine and alachor drinking water standard). One regulation actually cost 60 times as much as the $92 billion standard, but the estimate seemed out of line. Ibid., pp. 24–27. Breyer's analysis seeks ways to overcome vast inefficiencies in regulations, by placing such extreme bad bets at the top end of the cost distribution. Since only statistical losses are involved in regulatory policy choices, such reforms are likely to be politically and psychologically easier to adopt than would decisions to withhold benefits from the identified bad bets who are our subject.

18. Lisa A. Prosser and others, "Cost-Effectiveness of Cholesterol-Lowering Therapies according to Selected Patient Characteristics," *Annals of Internal Medicine* 132, no. 10 (May 16, 2000): 769–79.

19. See, generally, Peter H. Schuck, "The Graying of Civil Rights Law: The Age Discrimination Act of 1975," *Yale Law Journal* 89 (1979): 27.

20. Henry J. Aaron and William B. Schwartz with Melissa Cox, *Can We Say No? The Challenge of Rationing Health Care* (Brookings, 2005), pp. 36–37 and 42.

21. Philip G. Peters Jr., "Health Care Rationing and Disability Rights," *Indiana Law Journal* 70 (1995): 501–05.

22. Eric Nagourny, "Transplants: For Kidneys, Age Matters Little," *New York Times*, March 15, 2005, sec. F, p. 6.

23. Personal communication from Samuel Osher, MD, Harvard University Health Services, July, 6, 2006.

24. James Lubitz, James Beebe, and Colin Baker, "Longevity and Medical Expenditures," *New England Journal of Medicine* 332 (April 10, 1995): 999–1003.

25. All figures are from James D. Lubitz and Gerald F. Riley, "Trends in Medicare Payments in the Last Year of Life," *New England Journal of Medicine* 328 (April 15, 1993): 1092–96.

26. See Daniel Altman, "How to Save Medicare? Die Sooner," *New York Times*, February 27, 2005, Business sec., p. 1 (citing Dr. Gail Wilensky, Project HOPE).

27. Lawrence Schneiderman and Nancy Jecker, *Wrong Medicine: Doctors, Patients, and Futile Treatments* (Johns Hopkins University Press, 1995), p. 14.

28. Bernard Lo, *Resolving Ethical Dilemmas: A Guide for Clinicians* (Baltimore, Md.: Williams and Wilkins, 1995), pp. 73–81.

29. Ibid.

30. See John A. Robertson, "Schiavo and Its (In)Significance," Public Law Research Paper 86 (University of Texas Law School, 2006) (ssrn.com/abstract=881112).

31. This oft-quoted threshold originated from Lawrence J. Schneiderman and others, "Medical Futility: Its Meaning and Ethical Implications," *Annals of Internal Medicine* 112 (1990): 949. They defined quantitative futility as a situation when physicians determine that a particular medical treatment has been useless in the past 100 (presumably similarly situated) cases, through empirical data, information from other physicians, or personal experience.

32. See, for example, "Medical Futility in End-of-Life Care: Report of the Council on Ethical and Judicial Affairs," *JAMA* 281 (1999): 937.

33. See, for example, Rurik Löfmark and Tore Nilstun, "Conditions and Consequences of Medical Futility—From Literature Review to a Clinical Model," *Journal of Medical Ethics* 28 (2002): 115–19.

34. Ibid., 115, 117. The authors do acknowledge that these differing decisions maintained within the same article "may reflect the complexity of the situation arising when trying to decide who should decide: the doctor or patient." Ibid., 118.

35. Catherine M. Breen and others, "Conflict Associated with Decisions to Limit Life-Sustaining Treatment in Intensive Care Units," *Journal of General Internal Medicine* 16 (2001): 283.

36. Ezekiel J. Emanuel, "Managed Care, Hospice Use, Site of Death, and Medical Expenditures in the Last Year of Life," *Archives of Internal Medicine* 162 (2002): 1722, 1727.

37. Linda L. Emanuel and Ezekiel J. Emanuel, "The Economics of Dying: The Illusion of Cost Savings at the End of Life," *New England Journal of Medicine* 330 (1994): 540.

38. Ezekiel J. Emanuel, "Cost Savings at the End of Life: What Do the Data Show?" *JAMA* 275 (1996): 1907–14. This meta-analysis of various studies published in the early to mid-1990s notes that despite the variable methodologies, patient populations, and quality of the studies, the 25 to 40 percent figure had reasonable consensus.

39. Laura Esserman and others, "Potentially Ineffective Care: A New Outcome to Assess the Limits of Critical Care," *JAMA* 274 (1995): 1544.

40. Simon Atkinson and others, "Identification of Futility in Intensive Care," *Lancet* 344 (1994): 1203.

41. Thomas J. Prendergast and John M. Luce, "Increasing Incidence of Withholding and Withdrawal of Life Support from the Critically Ill," *American Journal of Respiratory and Critical Care Medicine* 155 (1997): 15.

42. Thomas J. Prendergast, Michael T. Classens, and John M. Luce, "A National Survey of End-of-Life Care for Critically Ill Patients," *American Journal of Respiratory and Critical Care Medicine* 158 (1998): 1165.

43. Gina Kolata, "Medicare Says It Will Pay, but Patients Say 'No Thanks,'" *New York Times*, March 3, 2006, p. C1.

44. Ibid.

45. Ibid.

46. We thank Dr. Samuel Osher for this example. We assume that few patients would make their decisions on the basis of the additional information that such a choice would free up the resources for better bets.

47. See Altman, "How to Save Medicare? Die Sooner." Apparently, there is little research about whether hospice care saves money. Ibid.

48. See, generally, Peter H. Schuck, "Rethinking Informed Consent," *Yale Law Journal* 103 (1994): 899.

49. Donald Berwick, "As Good as It Should Get: Making Health Care Better in the New Millennium" (Cambridge, Mass.: Institute for Healthcare Improvement, 1998) (www.ihi.org/NR/rdonlyres/2C93F14E-164B-4ACF-992E-BFF7235F53E7/0/AsGood-AsItShouldGet.pdf).

50. The most extensive studies have been undertaken by a research group at Dartmouth. They found that higher-spending regions of the country received approximately 60 percent more care, with no gains in outcomes (www.annals.org/cgi/content/full/138/4/288).

51. See, for example, Ron Winslow, "Care Varies Widely at Top Medical Centers," *Wall Street Journal*, May 16, 2006, p. D1.

52. Profit here includes not only direct payment to the physician for doing a more elaborate procedure, such as a cesarean section (C-section) instead of a vaginal delivery, but also avoiding low-probability but costly malpractice claims, including unjustified claims resulting from a bad outcome after the vaginal delivery. Defensive medicine is frequently cited as producing bad bets, that is, inducing procedures or treatments that offer

little or negative medical benefit, such as a medical test that is exceedingly unlikely to yield any valuable information but protects against a malpractice claim. Some defensive medicine protects against such claims because many bad outcomes are inevitable, yet it is difficult to show that a bad outcome was not due to a mistake. For example, with some forms of retardation due to genes, it may be impossible to show at present that they were not due to oxygen deprivation during delivery.

53. Gary L. Gaumer and Joanna Stavins, "Medicare Use in the Last Ninety Days of Life," *Health Services Research* 26, no. 6 (February 1992): 725–42.

54. Michael E. Porter and Elizabeth Olmstead Teisberg, *Redefining Health Care, Creating Value-Based Competition on Results* (Harvard Business School Press, 2006). See particularly pages 127–34 for an explanation of how good outcome data were produced for a variety of conditions and procedures.

55. See Alan S. Gerber and Eric M. Patashnik, *Promoting the General Welfare: New Perspectives on Government Performance* (Brookings, forthcoming), chapter 3; John Carey, "Medical Guesswork," *Business Week*, May 29, 2006, p. 72.

56. See Alex Berenson, "Cancer Drugs Offer Hope, but at Huge Expense," *New York Times*, July 12, 2005, p. A1.

57. See Laura Johannes, "For Some Transplant Patients, Diseased Hearts Are Lifesavers," *Wall Street Journal*, April 14, 2005, p. A1.

58. Katrina A. Bramstedt, "Aortic Valve Replacement in the Elderly: Frequently Indicated Yet Frequently Denied," *Gerontology* 49 (2003): 46.

59. Consider two recent examples. In the first, the German Constitutional Court overruled a government decision that had denied coverage to an individual with a rare disease for which the only treatment was both highly experimental and very costly. The court ruled that the government had a legal duty to cover the cost where no conventional treatment existed and a positive outcome could not be reasonably excluded. Decision of December 6, 2005, 1 BvR 347/98. In the second, the British health service denied a woman with HER2 early-stage breast cancer the use of Herceptin, a drug that costs roughly $40,000 per year, which some studies show is helpful for her condition. Her local health service ruled that it would only be given to early-stage patients in "exceptional circumstances." She sued and won. The court saw no way to distinguish among patients "on the basis of exceptional clinical circumstances." Noting the many potential users of this drug, the chief executive of the NHS (National Health Service) Confederation, presumably thinking in terms of the targeting approach, stated that "every pound spent on one expensive drug or treatment is potentially at the expense of other patients." Sarah Lyall, "Court Backs Briton's Right to a Costly Drug," *New York Times*, April 13, 2006, p. A3.

60. Sarah Lyall, "Court Backs Briton's Right to a Costly Drug."

61. Bruce Ackerman and Anne Alstott, *The Stakeholder Society* (Yale University Press, 1999), pp. 212–13.

62. Such choices vaguely approximate the types of choices that Rawls considered when citizens make decisions behind the veil of ignorance.

63. See, for example, Gardiner Harris, "Money for Vaccinating Children Is Diverted for Experimental Adult Flu Shots, Officials Say," *New York Times*, December 16, 2004, p. A28.

64. Jacob S. Hacker, "False Positive," *New Republic*, August 16 and 23, 2004, pp. 14, 16 (citing research of Julia Lynch). See also Gardiner Harris, "Money for Vaccinating Children Is Diverted for Experimental Adult Flu Shots, Officials Say."

65. See, for example, our discussion above of the use of statins to lower cholesterol, which tends to not be given to low-risk groups, even though they receive some positive benefit from it. With some other drug treatments, the system fails to avoid bad bets. Doctors have a choice in drugs given after heart attacks to reduce future risk, namely streptokinase versus the much more expensive TPA. Although TPA offers significant additional benefits to some groups, but virtually none to others, it is almost always the drug that is prescribed. Personal communication from David Cutler, professor of economics, Harvard University, July 6, 2006.

66. See Mark Kelman and Gillian Lester, *Jumping the Queue: An Inquiry into the Legal Treatment of Students with Learning Disabilities* (Harvard University Press, 1997).

67. For an extended discussion of age discrimination, see Peter H. Schuck, "The Graying of Civil Rights Law."

68. U.S. Department of Education Press Release, "Secretary Spellings Announces New Student Loan Default Rate," September 14, 2005 (www.ed.gov/news/pressreleases/2005/09/09142005.html). Fortunately, default rates have been moving in the right direction. In 2003, apparently the latest year for which figures are available, default rates were only 4.5 percent, down from its peak of 22.4 percent of student borrowers in 1990. Jon Marcus, "Debt Up but Defaults Down," *Times Higher Education Supplement* 1711 (September 30, 2005): 13. Trends in default rates are also available on the U.S. Department of Education website (www.ed.gov/offices/OSFAP/defaultmanagement/defaultrates.html [accessed March 2006]).

69. See Denise Grady, "2 Women, 2 Deaths and an Ethical Quandary," *New York Times,* July 15, 2003, p. F1.

70. Jonathan Kahn, "How a Drug Becomes 'Ethnic': Law, Commerce, and the Production of Racial Categories in Medicine," *Yale Journal of Health Policy, Law, and Ethics* 4 (2004): 1. See also "Not a Black and White Question," *Economist*, April 15, 2006, pp. 79–80.

71. In addition to the possible unfairness of evicting families that cannot control the behavior of the member, one concern is that the policy will lead to underreporting of criminal behavior. See, for example, Evi Schueller, "Note: *HUD* v. *Rucker*, Unconscionable Due Process for Public Housing Tenants," *U.C. Davis Law Review* 37 (2004): 1175, 1199.

Chapter 5

1. Robert J. Sampson and Dawn Jeglum Bartusch, "Legal Cynicism and (Subcultural?) Tolerance of Deviance: The Neighborhood Context of Racial Differences," *Law & Society Review* 32 (1998): 777.

2. Malcolm Gladwell, "Million-Dollar Murray," *New Yorker,* February 13 and 20, 2006, pp. 96–103.

3. Ibid.

4. An unusual exception, where the law makes no such distinctions, is a three-strikes law. Such laws permanently remove from society bad apples convicted of three felonies, without differentiating according to the nature of those felonies. Whether such laws succeed in identifying the truly rotten apples is questionable.

5. Personal communication from Lee Anne Fennell, professor, University of Illinois, College of Law, February 12, 2006.

6. Personal communication from Ron Haskins, senior fellow, Brookings Institution, March 10, 2005.

7. See James F. Blumstein, "The Fraud and Abuse Statute in an Evolving Healthcare Marketplace: Life in the Healthcare Speakeasy," *American Journal of Law and Medicine* 22 (1996): 205.

8. James Barron, "Many Saw Free Air-Conditioner In Post-9/11 Clean-Air Program," *New York Times*, November 2, 2004, p. A1.

9. Eric Lipton, "Study Finds Huge Fraud In the Wake Of Hurricanes," *New York Times*, June 14, 2006, p. A21.

10. See, for example, Julie Creswell, "Testing for Silicosis Comes Under Scrutiny in Congress," *New York Times*, March 8, 2006, p. C3.

11. *New York Times*, "Social Security Overpayments," October 19, 2004, p. A3.

12. See, for example, Daisy F. Reed and Caroline Kirkpatrick, "Disruptive Students in the Classroom: A Review of the Literature" (Richmond, Va.: Metropolitan Educational Research Consortium, 1998); "The MetLife Survey of the American Teacher, 2001: Key Elements of Quality" (New York: MetLife, 2001), pp. 39, 42, 58.

13. One economic model of this relationship, which considers both costs and educational value, finds that when disrupters are absent or unlikely to be present, the optimal class size is larger. This indicates that disruptive students impose, in addition, the direct financial cost of needing to hire more teachers. Edward P. Lazear, "Educational Production," *Quarterly Journal of Economics* 116 (2001): 777–803.

14. *Disruptive* can include rudeness to or defiance of teachers, verbal insults, bullying, and frequently entering the classroom late. *Nonserious violence* can include kicking, biting, hitting, shoving, grabbing, and vandalism. *Violence* can include weapons possession, threatened assault, and fist fighting. *Criminal violence* can include aggravated assaults. See Jill F. DeVoe and others, *Indicators of School Crime and Safety: 2002* (Washington: U.S. Department of Education, National Center for Education Statistics, November 2002), p. ix; Amanda K. Miller and Kathryn Chandler, *Violence in U.S. Public Schools: 2000 School Survey on Crime and Safety* (Washington: U.S. Department of Education, National Center for Education Statistics, October 2003), pp. 4, 19–20.

15. DeVoe and others, *Indicators of School Crime and Safety: 2002*, p. ix. Seven percent of all students responding to a survey felt that they were not at all safe at school compared with 2 percent of teachers. The teachers were from grades K–12, and the students were in grades 7–12. "The MetLife Survey of the American Teacher, 2001," pp. 39–42.

16. Miller and Chandler, *Violence in U.S. Public Schools*, p. 20.

17. Ibid., pp. v, 39, 57, 58. But see Fox Butterfield, "Crime in Schools Fell Sharply Over the 10 Years Ended '02," *New York Times*, November 30, 2004, p. A21. Despite the decline, "bullying, violent crime, drinking and drugs remained a serious problem at many schools."

18. See Susan Saulny, "Noncrime Disturbances Rise at Tough Schools," *New York Times*, August 3, 2005, p. B8.

19. David M. Herszenhorn, "Data on Violence in City Schools Is Questioned," *New York Times*, June 13, 2006, p. B6.

20. Public Agenda, "Teaching Interrupted: Do Discipline Policies in Today's Schools Foster the Common Good?" (New York: May 2004) .

21. Brian Kleiner and others, *Public Alternative Schools and Programs for Students at Risk of Education Failure: 2000–01* (Washington: U.S. Department of Education, National Center for Education Statistics, September 2002), pp. 6, 10, 23, 27. The few evaluations of these schools present mixed results.

22. See Elissa Gootman, "Gotbaum Says City is Failing to Remove Violent Students," *New York Times*, January 14, 2005, p. B2, for a discussion on the Public Advocate's report that many multiple and violent offenders are not being removed.

23. Richard Arum, *Judging School Discipline: The Crisis of Moral Authority* (Harvard University Press, 2003). See also Kevin Brady, "Zero Tolerance or (In)tolerance Policies? Weaponless School Violence, Due Process, and the Law of Student Suspensions and Expulsions," *Brigham Young University Education and Law Journal* 1 (2002): 159; Anne Proffit Dupre, "A Study of Double Standards, Discipline, and Disabled Students," *Washington Law Review* 75 (2000): 1.

24. 419 U.S. 565 (1975).

25. This paragraph is based on Julie Underwood, "The 30th Anniversary of *Goss v. Lopez*," *Education Law Reporter* 198 (2005): 795, 798–801.

26. The Individuals with Disabilities Education Act (IDEA) is codified at 20 U.S.C. Sec. 1400.

27. Advancement Project and Civil Rights Project at Harvard University, *Opportunities Suspended: The Devastating Consequences of Zero Tolerance and School Discipline*, report from a National Summit on Zero Tolerance, June 15–16, 2000, Washington, D.C., p. 48 and Appendix III. Grounds for suspension include disruptive behavior, assault, possession of a paging device, hate violence, extortion, violence against a school official, sexual harassment, tobacco and alcohol use, gang membership, disobedience, defiance of authority, and profanity. Only ten of the forty-nine states with applicable statutory guidelines count "disruptive behavior" or "continued defiance of authority" as a ground for expulsion, although individual schools' policies may differ. Most expulsion guidelines focus instead on students who are found to possess firearms or other weapons.

28. See the U.S. Department of Education website: OCR Elementary and Secondary School Survey: 2000 (vistademo.beyond2020.com/ocr2000r/).

29. More specifically, data from the Office of Civil Rights (OCR) estimate that a total of 83,108 students faced long-term suspension or removal (with no cessation of services). The OCR data are available online (vistademo.beyond2020.com/ocr2000r). *Long-*

term placements refer to those placements that are used to discipline students for more than ten days.

30. Government Accounting Office (since 2004, Government Accountability Office, GAO), *Student Discipline: Individuals with Disabilities Education Act* (January 2001), pp. 15–20, 29.

31. For a case study of one particularly intrusive decree in New York City's special education program, *Jose P. v. Ambach*, see Ross Sandler and David Schoenbrod, *Democracy By Decree: What Happens When Courts Run Government* (Yale University Press, 2003), chapter 3.

32. Irene R. Beattie, Richard Arum, and Josipa Roksa, "Zero Tolerance School Discipline and Student Rights: Changes in Court Climates and Legal Contestation, 1960–2002," paper presented at the annual meeting of the American Sociological Association, San Francisco, California, August 2004.

33. See Elissa Gotman, "Gotbaum Says City Is Failing To Remove Violent Students," *New York Times*, January 14, 2005, p. B2.

34. GAO, *Special Education, Clearer Guidance Would Enhance Implementation of Federal Disciplinary Provisions*, report to the ranking minority member, U.S. Senate, Committee on Health, Education, Labor and Pensions, May 2003, pp. 7–11. Homebound placements are similar to at-home suspension, but with remediation, tutoring, and related services.

35. Susan Saulny, "Students Sue School System, Claiming Denial of Education," *New York Times*, November 21, 2004, p. B3.

36. See William S. Gilliam, "Prekindergarteners Left Behind: Expulsion Rates in State Prekindergarten Programs," Foundation for Child Policy Brief Series 3 (New Haven, Conn.: Yale University Child Study Center, May 2005) (www.fcd-us.org/PDFs/National-PreKExpulsionPaper03.02_new.pdf). The expulsion rate in child care programs in Massachusetts was thirteen times higher than the rate in K–12 programs nationwide. William S. Gilliam and G. Shahar, "Preschool and Child Care Expulsion and Suspensions: Rates and Predictors in One State," *Infants and Young Children* 19 (2006): 228–45.

37. In the literature, *alternative schools* and *alternative education programs* are interchangeable terms. Descriptively, the latter is broader in scope, encompassing alternative arrangements located within a traditional school and alternative schools located off-site. Unless otherwise stated, we use the broader term "programs."

38. Advancement Project and Civil Rights Project at Harvard University, "Opportunities Suspended: The Devastating Consequences of Zero Tolerance and School Discipline," p. 14 and Appendix III (www.civilrightsproject.harvard.edu/research/discipline/opport_suspended.php#fullreport).

39. Robert Barr and William Parrett, *Hope Fulfilled for At-Risk and Violent Youth: K–12 Programs that Work,* 2d ed. (Needham Heights, Mass.: Allyn and Bacon, 2001); Garry Natriello and others, *Schooling Disadvantaged Children: Racing Against Catastrophe* (New York: Teachers College Press, 1990); Mary Anne Raywid, "The Mounting Case for Schools of Choice," in *Public Schools by Choice: Expanding Opportunities for Parents, Students, and Teachers,* edited by Joe Nathan (Bloomington, Ind.: Meyer Stone Books, 1998); Gary Wehlage and others, *Reducing the Risk: Schools as Communities of Support* (New York: Falmer Press, 1989).

40. Advancement Project and Civil Rights Project at Harvard University, *Opportunities Suspended,* p. 14. The authors supply only anecdotal evidence, which is rampant in the literature. See Cheryl M. Lange and Sandra J. Sletten, *Alternative Education: A Brief History and Research Synthesis,* report prepared for Project Forum (Alexandria, Va.: National Association of State Directors of Special Education, February 2002), p. 2. The dearth of assessment data stems in part from the widely varying definitions and implementations of these programs. As noted above, New York City officials cited the pending legal challenge to its programs as a basis for refusing to discuss them with the authors.

41. U.S. Department of Education, *Creating Safe and Drug Free Schools: An Action Guide* (September 1996), p. 65.

42. Ibid. The cost data appear to be for the 1990s; efforts to confirm and update these were unsuccessful.

43. AFT website (www.aft.org/topics/discipline/alternative.htm [accessed March 2005]).

44. Julie Underwood, "The 30th Anniversary of *Goss v. Lopez.*"

45. As one reason for their recalcitrance, New York officials cited a pending legal challenge to its system for removing disruptive students and providing alternative schooling. The lawsuit is *E.B.* v. *New York City Board of Education,* CV-02-5118 (CPS).

46. Interview with Ricardo E. Morales, general counsel of the New York City Housing Authority (NYCHA), and his staff, March 10, 2006. Personal communication with Ricardo E. Morales, March 15, 2006.

47. U.S. Department of Housing and Urban Development (HUD), *In the Crossfire: The Impact of Gun Violence on Public Housing Communities* (1999), p.15. The study from the Bureau of Justice Statistics is Carol J. DeFrances and Steven K. Smith, *Perceptions of Neighborhood Crime* (U.S. Department of Justice, April 1998). There were no data on the number of gun-related homicides in the other 34 public housing communities.

48. HUD, *In the Crossfire,* pp. 16–18.

49. Ibid., p. 17. This sample may not be nationally representative.

50. Dan Nnamdi Mbulu, "Affordable Housing: How Effective Are Existing Federal Laws in Addressing the Housing Needs of Lower Income Families?" *American University Journal of Gender, Social Policy, and the Law* 8, no. 2 (2000): 396.

51. HUD, *In the Crossfire,* pp. 21, 25. Modernization needs in public housing were estimated at more than $20 billion in 1999.

52. Even the briefs and decision in the *Rucker* case, discussed immediately below, lacked such data; instead the Court treated public housing crime as an undisputed crisis that Congress had acknowledged.

53. 535 U.S. 125 (2002).

54. Kimberly E. O'Leary, "Dialogue, Perspective and Point of View as Lawyering Method: A New Approach to Evaluating Anti-Crime Measures in Subsidized Housing," *Washington University Journal of Urban and Contemporary Problems* 49 (1996): 133, 142.

55. Interview with Lisa Walker Scott, executive director and general counsel, Housing and Development Law Institute, Washington, D.C., March 22, 2006. The discussion that follows draws on interviews and a telephone conversation with Ricardo E. Morales, gen-

eral counsel of the New York City Housing Authority and his staff (see note 46). We also interviewed officials in New Haven's program. Although we make no claims about the representativeness of the programs in these cities, our interviews confirmed that the nature of the problem of bad apples in both cities is similar even though the scales of the two programs are vastly different. In only a few instances, noted below, did the New Haven interviews add to the picture presented by the New York City program.

56. NYCHA Fact Sheet, revised December 15, 2005.

57. Interview with Maureen Novak and Kate Sylvester, New Haven Housing Authority, February 1, 2006.

58. Ibid.

59. *Escalera* v. *New York Housing Authority*, 924 F. Supp. 1323 (S.D. New York 1996). The litigation history recounted in the text is taken from this decision.

60. McKinney's Consolidated Laws of New York Annotated, Real Property Law, Chapter 50, Article 7, Section 231 (Eagan, Minnesota: Thomson/West Publishing, 2005).

61. NYCHA estimates the annual cost of Operation Safe Housing to be approximately $200,000, mostly due to the additional hearing officer and support staff. This does not include the opportunity cost, which is largely the diversion of the agency's attorneys from other tasks. Operation Safe Housing does not diminish any of the procedural protections to tenants.

62. This barment process has been upheld by the Supreme Court against a First Amendment challenge, *Virginia* v. *Hicks*, 539 U.S. 113 (2003).

63. The description that follows draws upon interviews with Patrick Markee, counsel to the Coalition for the Homeless, New York City, March 3, 2006, and Clarke Bruno, general counsel of the New York City Department of Homeless Services, and his staff, March 24, 2006.

64. This is an explicit concern of the New York City homelessness program. Leslie Kaufman, "State Revamps Plan to Give Assistance To Homeless," *New York Times*, December 11, 2004, p. B1 (quoting the commissioner of homeless services); Michael Cragg and Brendan O'Flaherty, "Do Homeless Shelter Conditions Determine Shelter Population? The Case of the Dinkins Deluge," *Journal of Urban Economics* 46 (1999): 37.

65. *Callahan* v. *Carey*, Supreme Court of New York, County of New York (Index No. 42582/79, consent decree entered August 1981). See also *Callahan* v. *Carey*, 307 A.D.2d 150; 762 N.Y.S.2d 349; 2003 N.Y. App.Div. LEXIS 6452 (First Dept, App. Div., 2003).

66. For the background as of July 2005, see Leslie Kaufman, "City Is Starting to Remove Rule Breakers from Shelters," *New York Times*, July 20, 2005, p. B1.

67. See Lawrence Sherman and others, *Preventing Crime: What Works, What Doesn't, What's Promising* (U.S. Department of Justice, 1997), pp. 10-8, 10-9; Office of Justice Programs, *Blueprints for Violence Preventions* (U.S. Department of Justice, 2004), p. 60.

68. Lawrence Sherman and others, *Preventing Crime*, p. 10-4.

69. National Institutes of Health, press release, "Panel Finds that Scare Tactics for Violence Are Harmful," October 15, 2004 (www.nih.gov/news/pr/oct2004/od-15.htm [accessed March 2005]).

70. Office of Justice Programs, *Blueprints for Violence Preventions*, p. 59. "Intervening early in the developmental life course is critical for interrupting negative socialization processes that may place a child on a path that may involve antisocial behavior, dropping out of school, and poor adult socialization."

71. *New York Times*, "'Get Tough' Youth Programs Are Ineffective, Panel Says," October 17, 2004, p. 26. The National Institutes of Health finds that these programs bring together young people who are inclined toward violence and teach one another how to commit more crime.

72. Robert Martinson, "What Works? Questions and Answers about Prison Reform," *Public Interest* 35 (Spring 1974): 25.

73. David Farabee, *Rethinking Rehabilitation: Why Can't We Reform Our Criminals?* (Washington: American Enterprise Institute, 2005), pp. 5–6.

74. Patrick A. Langan and David J. Levin, *Recidivism of Prisoners Released in 1994*, Bureau of Justice Statistics Special Report NCJ 193427 (U.S. Department of Justice, June 2002).

75. GAO, *Adult Drug Courts: Evidence Indicates Recidivism Reductions and Mixed Results for Other Outcomes* (February 2005), p. 7.

76. Ibid.

77. For a recent study examining expulsions from prekindergarten programs, see Walter S. Gilliam, "Prekindergarteners Left Behind."

78. Because of the pending *E.B.* lawsuit against New York City's system of alternative schools, cited in note 45, we were unable to gather data on this important question.

79. *Governor's Welfare/Medicaid Revision Proposals*, Hearings of the Senate Finance Committee, 103rd Cong., 2nd sess., 26 February 1996. For a discussion of resignations from the U.S. Department of Health and Human Services by top officials Peter Edelman and Mary Jo Bane, see E.J. Dionne Jr., "Resigning on Principle," *Washington Post*, September 17, 1996, p. A15. For some other examples of vilification, see Ron Haskins, "Welfare Check," *Wall Street Journal*, July 27, 2006, p. A12.

80. For the most current, comprehensive review of the evidence, see Ron Haskins, *Work over Welfare: The Inside Story of the 1996 Welfare Reform Law* (Brookings, forthcoming 2006). The data on domestic violence appear in Jennifer Nou and Christopher D. Timmins, "How Do Changes in Welfare Law Affect Domestic Violence? An Analysis of Connecticut Towns, 1990–2000," *Journal of Legal Studies*, forthcoming 2006.

81. Leslie Kaufman, "It's a Trend: Births Out of Wedlock Are Falling Statewide," *New York Times*, October 2, 2004, p. B1. New York officials consider welfare reform the most important factor in explaining the decline.

Chapter 6

1. For a discussion of collaborative governance arrangements, see John D. Donahue and Richard J. Zeckhauser, "Public-Private Collaboration," in *Oxford Handbook of Public Policy*, edited by Robert Goodin, Michael Moran, and Martin Rein (Oxford University Press, forthcoming 2006).

2. See the website of the Academy of the Pacific Rim (www.pacrim.org/test_scores.htm).

3. Virginia Postrel, "The Poverty Puzzle," *New York Times Magazine*, March 19, 2006, p. 12. See also Jeffrey D. Sachs, "Net Gains," *New York Times*, April 29, 2006, p. A11.

4. See Albert L. Nichols and Richard J. Zeckhauser, "Targeting Transfers through Restrictions on Recipients," *American Economic Review* 72, no. 2 (May 1982): 372–77.

5. Guido Calabresi, *The Cost of Accidents: A Legal and Economic Analysis* (Yale University Press, 1970).

6. See Frederick Schauer and Richard J. Zeckhauser, "On the Degree of Confidence for Adverse Decisions," *Journal of Legal Studies* 25 (January 1996): 27–52.

7. Mathematically inclined readers will understand why the slope of the curve at either A^* or B^* is $-1/2$. By contrast, if Type I errors were twice as costly as Type II errors, the appropriate point on the curve would be the one where the slope is -2. Obviously, when Type I errors become relatively more expensive, we choose to get fewer of them.

8. For a discussion of the first known and acknowledged case of an innocent man being found guilty and executed, see Bob Herbert, "Convicted, Executed, Not Guilty," *New York Times*, July 14, 2005, p. A25.

9. Peter H. Schuck, "Rethinking Informed Consent," *Yale Law Journal* 103 (1994): 899.

10. The January-February 2005 issue of *Health Affairs* (24, no. 1) focused on evidence-based medicine. This is reassuring but also disturbing. What were doctors practicing in the past?

11. See Mark Kelman and Gillian Lester, *Jumping the Queue: An Inquiry into the Legal Treatment of Students with Learning Disabilities* (Harvard University Press, 1997).

12. We are indebted to Howard Husock, Kennedy School, Harvard University, for this suggestion in a personal communication, August 8, 2005.

13. The authors take particular pride in the EITC, since they proposed a wage subsidy for low-income working poor in 1970, five years before the EITC was enacted. See Peter Schuck and Richard Zeckhauser, "An Alternative to the Nixon Income Maintenance Plan," *Public Interest* 19 (Spring 1970): 120–30.

14. Doron Teichman, "The Market for Criminal Justice: Federalism, Crime Control, and Jurisdictional Competition," *Michigan Law Review* 103 (June 2005). See particularly footnote 87.

15. The standard "7(a)" SBA loan program offers the lender a guarantee of 85 percent, leaving lenders at risk for the remainder (www.sba.gov/financing/subfiles/guaranty_percents.html).

Two types of government-guaranteed student loan programs exist: the Federal Direct Student Loans (FDSL) program and the Federal Family Education Loan Program (FFELP). In the former program, the government guarantees 100 percent of the loan. The latter program involves private lenders lending money to students through their colleges and through a state or nonprofit guarantee agency. With federal funding, these guaranty agencies generally insure the lender for 98 percent of the unpaid amount of defaulted loans. See, for example, GAO, *Federal Student Loans*, January 2002, pp. 4–5.

16. *New York Times*, "Pork 1, Antiterrorism 0," June 2, 2006, p. A20.

17. See, generally, Cass R. Sunstein, "Group Judgments: Statistical Means, Deliberation, and Information Markets," *New York University Law Review* 80 (2005): 962; Robert W. Hahn and Paul C. Tetlock, "A New Approach for Regulating Information Markets," AEI-Brookings Joint Center for Regulatory Studies (December 2004).

18. 424 U.S. 319 (1976), pp. 334–35.

19. Jerry L. Mashaw, *Bureaucratic Justice: Managing Social Security Disability Claims* (Yale University Press, 1983), pp. 21–23.

20. See Judge Henry J. Friendly's famous article, "Some Kind of Hearing," *University of Pennsylvania Law Review* 123 (1975): 1267.

21. But see Susan Saulny, "Students Sue School System, Claiming Denial of Education," *New York Times*, November 21, 2004, p. B3. Former juvenile offenders and delinquents claim that the system fails to return students to school after their detention.

22. For some different approaches to this goal, see Peter Schuck, ed., *Foundations of Administrative Law*, 2d ed. (New York: Foundation Press, 2004), pp. 340–75.

Chapter 7

1. For example, Viagra treats impotence, but it is also used by some to enhance sexual function. See Robert Pear, "Dispute Over Medicare Plan to Cover Erectile Treatments," *New York Times*, February 2, 2005, p. A13. Without any practicable way to verify their reasons for seeking the drugs, a second-best screening mechanism may be to require people to declare their reasons under penalty of perjury, even though some of them will lie.

2. In a sense, we wish to compute the Gini coefficient for unfortunate outcomes. If a tiny percentage of recipients account for a large percentage of the problem, as chapter 5 showed to be likely, then the coefficient is high, and a strong argument exists for additional sorting of the recipient population. For the problem of bad bets, the Gini coefficient would be attached to the ratio of dollars spent to dollars of benefit.

3. See the discussion of "moral hazard in compassion" and "moral hazard due to proximity" in chapter 4.

4. See the discussion of cesareans in chapter 4.

5. In the quite different realm of valuing environmental losses in response to surveys, studies show that people are willing to pay almost as much to save 100 birds as 1,000 birds. In like spirit, the discomfort from not treating 1,000 people for a disease may be perceived as much less than 1,000 times as great as not treating the single person with an equivalently serious disease.

6. Alternative programs could also reduce the incidence of costly and discipline-chilling lawsuits against the schools, although the *E.B.* litigation challenging alternative programs in New York City, noted in chapter 5, may make this hope a vain one.

Index

Cost-effectiveness research, 68. *See also* Benefit-cost test

Costs: disproportionate costs of bad apples or bad bets, 130; of errors and appeals, 112–16; of screening and analysis to choose who receives benefits, 106–07, 131; of social programs, 28–32

"Creaming" as method of choosing who receives benefits, 106, 117

Crime: in public housing, 87–88; three-strikes rule and predicting behavior changes, 120, 127. *See also* Violence

Critical care and QALY analysis, 54

Data collection, strengthening of, 116–17, 129–31

Decision theory and lower error costs, 126

Definitions, 7–9; problems of employing, 16–17

Department of. *See specific department*

Department of Housing and Urban Development v. *Rucker* (*2002*), 88

Disabled persons: educational rights of, 83–85; health care for, 20; and social programs, 101. *See also* SSI benefits

Domestic violence, 98

Downstream redistribution of benefits and costs, 42

Drought insurance, 32

Drug rehabilitation programs, 100, 108

Drug-related crime and public housing, 88–92

Drunken drivers and probability of harm, 77

Due process, 16, 96, 122–27, 136; and appeals process, 101–02, 125–26; and bad bets vs. bad apples, 115–16; and eligibility criteria, 102–06; and hearings for rebuttal, 124–25; and school discipline cases, 82–83; and

statement of reasons for classification, 124

Earned Income Tax Credit (EITC), 30, 33, 34, 35, 118

Elderly and U.S. social programs, 71. *See also* Age; Medicare

Eligibility determinations, 102–06, 117–20

Emphysema surgical treatment, 65

Entitlement programs, 105. *See also specific welfare program*

Environmental Protection Agency, 23

Equal protection, 16

Errors of exclusion and inclusion, 109–12; costs of, 127; losses due to sorting errors, 114–16; Type I and Type II errors, 106, 110–16

Escalera decree (*1971*), 90, 91, 92

Estimates to value statistical life, 50

Ethics. *See* Morality and bad apples

Eviction of nuisance tenants from public housing, 89–92

Export-your-problems strategy, 120

Expulsions from school, 82–85

Fairness, 17–20, 136. *See also* Due process

Federal deficit, 28

Fees for program participants, 104–05

Fiscal costs. *See* Costs

Food stamp program, 19–20, 33, 34–35

Fraud and abuse, 36, 37, 40, 79–80

Futile care and medical expenditures, 62–64, 65

Future research needs for better targeting, 131

Future trends for policymaking process, 127–28

GAO. *See* Government Accountability Office